GRACE:
GOD'S
WORK
ETHIC

Making connections between the gospel and weekday work

Paul G. Johnson

Judson Press® Valley Forge

GRACE: GOD'S WORK ETHIC

Copyright © 1985
Judson Press, Valley Forge, PA 19482-0851

Library of Congress Cataloging in Publication Data
Johnson, Paul G.
    Grace, God's work ethic; making connections between
the gospel and weekday work
        Bibliography: p. 2
        Includes index.
        1. Work (Theology)   2. Laity. I. Title.
BT738.5.J64   1985   261.8'5   84-23336
ISBN 0-8170-1070-X

The name JUDSON PRESS is registered as a trademark in the U.S. Patent Office.
Printed in the U.S.A. ⊕

To my wife, Miriam,
whose example of
grace in the workplace
is a constant source
of inspiration.

Foreword

Paul G. Johnson has discovered a serious oversight in the Reformation churches: we have drifted into a new legalism that worships achievements. This has happened—in a very silent way—by our uncritically accepting the competitive basis of modern society. The sermon may talk, as the Reformers did, about "the tyranny of the law," but with little or no reference to how this tyranny today is in full power during the workdays of lay members.

This is to say that we in the Reformation churches have, on the decisive point, lost our central message: "Justification by faith without works." This message is clear and effective only if the accusing law is unveiled, unveiled at the point where it is accusing *today*. This point is now at a different place than it was in the sixteenth century.

The author of this book has put his finger on a central problem in the church. What Johnson has done, and done in an admirable way, is this: he has staked out a direction for future work in the church, the task of connecting the message of grace in Christ with the hard questions of the workplace.

Paul G. Johnson's book has an added quality that is educationally excellent. At the end of each chapter there are statements and questions that can be used as conversation starters.

Gustaf Wingren
Lund, Sweden

Contents

Preface

Since a preface is a personal word to the reader from the author, what follows are my reasons for writing this book. There are at least four, the first of which I have perceived from my own background and experience as a preacher.

What led to my growing awareness of the chasm between what I preached on Sunday and the reality of Monday is not clear to me, but I do recall becoming aware of standing in the pulpit and proclaiming God's Word with little thought of relating it to the daily work scene, where people spend much of their time. If I did enter the workplace in my sermon, it was to admonish the congregation to be "little Christs" there. In most sermons, however, there was no link whatsoever. The members of my congregation and I were in the same room but worlds apart. Even when the setting for the text was the first-century workplace from which Jesus drew a parable, I was inclined to duck the context and give it a spiritual meaning or application. Moreover, for years I never talked with people about their daily work, and taking their cue from my silence, they never brought it up in my presence.

The more I became aware of the lay world, however, the

more I realized that commentaries and sermon-help books did not help me to fill this void. Indeed, seed thoughts they provided only helped perpetuate it. During busy weeks these were the only books I had time to read although I had many others in my library. The pressure of getting ready for next Sunday's sermon made this seem like a necessity.

Then one day in 1972 a tome entitled *A Study of Generations* arrived; it was a gift to all Lutheran pastors from the Lutheran Brotherhood Insurance Corporation. Not only was its length formidable, but its message hit me like future shock, even though I was in the present. The message was that two-thirds of the folks in the pews on a Sunday morning had a law orientation to Christianity, despite the fact that they might have been exposed to the Good News of grace from the pulpit. It was as if a translation had been made in midair or something had filtered out the word of "grace" and replaced it with an unuttered exhortation to try harder. The more I wondered what was going on, the more I longed for the opportunity to do some exploring.

That opportunity came when I was asked to fill a position on a research staff for the Lutheran Church in America. My first assignment was to undertake a "theological climate" study with one main guideline—to build on prior studies.

As I read studies that were in the files, I found two that confirmed the finding in *A Study of Generations*. One was "Affirmations of Faith," a project completed in 1973. The other, conducted in 1977–1978, was part of a series called the "Lutheran Listening Post" (LLP). In both, the law-oriented two-thirds showed up again. In the LLP, for example, there was a question with seven options describing what faith means. Of the seven, only one included a reference to grace and only 34 percent of the lay respondents chose it, whereas 74 percent of the clergy respondents selected it. It seemed that a theological education made a difference.

What then caught my eye was the recommendation of over one thousand lay persons in the 1973 study. It was that "lay persons should be encouraged to compare openly the theology they hear in church with the operational theologies of everyday life." It was as if these lay persons were onto something but didn't say what it was. In any event, this recommendation seemed directly related to the theological climate in the church, and I decided to pursue it, especially since the results of the study stated that a number of theologians had affirmed the recommendation. They wanted to know where people were in their faith and perception.

It is obvious to many non-Lutherans that Lutherans have no corner on the understanding that the Good News of God's grace is free and unearned. However, it is reasonable to assume that such an emphasis would be central in Lutheran schools of theology and should also be central in their parish counterparts, Lutheran pulpits. Thus, to find something else at work in Lutheran pews suggests not only something powerful, but also something pervasive in the area of Christian faith and daily work. In this book we will refer to the effort to enter this area as a "clue search."

The first clues came in during a preliminary look at operational theology provided by members from four congregations. Based on the insights gained in this preliminary study, a questionnaire was created. Several key questions openly compared the grace emphasis heard in church with the meritorious performance emphasis of the workplace. Subsequently, more than four hundred lay persons from forty-six congregations took part in this Sherlock-Holmes-type theological investigation. One person summed up the feelings of one segment of participants when he wrote in his evaluation of the experience: "The questions were stimulating in that no one had asked us to analyze such issues before." Evidently a weekday influence can become so much a part of one's faith that it can be taken for granted as normal and never questioned. The majority, however, revealed a prior awareness of a gap between Sunday and Monday.

What the one thousand lay persons had discovered in 1973, the four hundred helped find words for in 1981. One more piece of a puzzle was in place. What people have heard about God through the church and even believe to be true is not necessarily what they believe about God during the week at work. The evidence indicates that the beliefs which the church affirmed during the Reformation and which it also teaches today are superceded at daily work by other, more deeply held beliefs.

Two factors make the evidence compelling. One, most participants were enrolled in their congregation's adult education courses or adult forums. If anyone had been open to the message of the gospel, it would have been they. The other factor is that most participants found the entry into the breach between their experience in church and their experience in daily work to be of such relevance to their faith that they shared their feelings with each other for months. Survey questions to which they responded in private were icebreakers for small group excursions that ranged far beyond the boundaries set by the questions themselves. We had encouraged this dimension but never expected it would take off as it did. The fact that this happened became part of the "data" that is inseparable from the content of the questions. It was as if we had unwittingly stumbled into some virgin territory and discovered that for most of the explorers it was exciting to be there.

It is also worthy of note that some highly positive responses to the study report were received from a number of Lutheran theologians. From seminaries in Gettysburg and Philadelphia, Chicago and St. Paul, Berkeley and Columbia (South Carolina), scholars wrote concerning the value of the study for the church. Along with their insights I also found some pages in *Creation and Gospel*, by Gustaf Wingren of Sweden, that provided the climate study with some additional perspective. Addressing the subject of legalism, Professor Wingren moves sequentially from Paul to Luther to our own time. While Paul and Luther confronted different forms of legalism, both were within the prevailing context of religion and the church. However, when Dr. Wingren comes to the twentieth century, he enters a different context. He writes, "Today it is necessary to raise the question of whether the factory worker in industrial society has not met the tyranny of the law in a form unknown in the sixteenth century."[1] He asserts that in practice many churches have accepted the competitive basis of technological society so uncritically as to have drifted into a new legalism that worships achievements.

Another factor leading to the writing of this book is activity in the workplace that borders on a "reformation." For example, Ford Motor Company announced early in 1984 that the annual performance reviews may be eliminated because of the harm they do to morale. This is but a sign of the new relationship between management and labor that is making itself known in a variety of corporations. It is one that makes people partners rather than adversaries. A new work ethic is emerging in America.

This phenomenon makes it easier to talk about daily work and its connection with the Good News of grace. The wall between them has a door in it. The force of the phenomenon is documented in the number of new books on managerial participation, which is also called "worker democracy." Harper & Row, for example, announced in 1983 that one book it had published in this area sold more copies in the first year than any other book had sold in that time period during the company's 166-year history. Such sales imply that while American corporations are in trouble, published thought on what to do about the problem is well received.

Although none of the books on worker democracy articulate the theological implications or faith-related issues that give them the "reformation" quality, the readers of these volumes, along with their friends, may be in church on Sunday. Thus, the church has an unprecedented opportunity to begin bridging the canyon between Sunday and Monday. The time is ripe for a theology of daily work written in nonjargonized language so that it can be shared directly from the pulpit, without translation.

That introduces one further reason for writing this book. When I, a parish pastor, searched my library for a volume to share with lay friends, I was often hard pressed to find one. It was as if the world of a clergy person was reflected not only in sermons but in the books purchased for reading. I believe this book, inspired by lay persons, could be used by lay persons in study groups, participants in workshops on the laity, or people on retreats. I think it would also speak to members of the future workforce who take courses in religion in college and would have particular relevance for students in theological schools. Toward that end there are statements and questions at the end of each chapter, lifted from the contents. Like the questions in the clue search, they can open the door to thoughts not included in the book. Reading the chapter before or after such sharing can provide background or a resource, but the statements and questions are not meant to test the reader's knowledge of what the book contains. They can be used this way, but at times a statement's wording is deliberately opposed to what the book says. The use of the questions and statements can best be implemented by asking people whether they agree or disagree and why. Each conversation group will share its own material. The leading of the Spirit into all truth never ends. From us there is no last word, only pauses between the lines.

Chapter 1

The Reformation's
Unintended Legacy

Someone said that a book is like light from a distant star. We see it five years after it has begun to shine. The subject matter of this volume has been on the way for twenty years. That is about how long it has been since I first visited a Protestant church building in New England, which was hemmed in on three sides by a factory. Walls of the factory were higher than those of the church and only ten feet away. They could have been ten miles high and light years away.

Although the factory was not operating on Sunday—noise was thus not a problem—ecclesiastical authorities felt that the congregation was doomed in that location. If it wished to grow, it should move to the suburbs. Besides that, the church looked funny where it was, as if God were caught in a trap.

For some reason the people did not want to move. Thus, when a pulpit vacancy developed there, church officials sent to the congregation a pastor who was known as a trouble shooter. His usual assignment was to go into a situation, knock heads together, and then leave, having accomplished the change in thinking that was sought, or so it was assumed.

The congregation did eventually move to the suburbs. It did

grow—numerically. However, what really happened represented an effort on the part of the "church" to move away from a
workplace. Ecclesiastical power succeeded in relocating bodies
on Sunday morning. What it did not succeed in doing was to
move people physically or psychologically away from their place
of work. It is no more possible to take the church out of the
workplace than to take the workplace out of the church, unless,
of course, the laity are excluded from the definition of "church."
This church became alienated from itself, not only laity from
clergy but laity from themselves and from their daily work.
Unfortunately, to move away from that place where people spent
much of their time was to move toward irrelevancy.

The movement of this congregation from the factory setting
is but a symbol of a separation that goes back a long time, far
enough to make the present alienation seem normal and thus
not alienation at all. Indeed, the subject matter of this book goes
back further than twenty years; but before we go there, I must
make one other stop along the way.

A seminary intern had just begun a year of serving in a
parish where he quickly discovered a difference between the
thinking he was being exposed to at school and the theology
that the lay people were sharing in their conversation. When
he returned to school for his senior year, he asked a professor
why there was so little preparation in the seminary for what lay
people think and believe. He was told, "We feel that you won't
spend much time studying theology once you are in the parish,
so we want to keep you at that task as long as you are here.
Besides, we feel that you will have plenty of time to learn about
the laity once you get there."

Two underlying assumptions emerge here, and they are
closely connected. One is that theology is supposed to be "done"
apart from the reality of business and industry. The other is that
the laity are not expected to understand the message; to understand it one must leave the scene of the congregation and
enroll in a school of theology. It is as if two kingdoms were
intentionally kept apart to avoid confusion. The "church" prov-
ince is that of the Word and the sacraments. Daily work is
something else.

This thinking or these assumptions go back to the 16th-
century Reformation and are part of the unintended legacy from

that period, one that could be called the "theological-school trickle down." Lay/clergy separation, of course, goes back further than that. However, since the Reformation was a response to the church theology and practices that went before it, what Protestants are and do relates to that brief interlude in a special way.

Separation of Church and Daily Work

The Good News of God's free and undeserved grace shared by the earliest Christians ceased being free and undeserved. By the sixteenth century it was sold to help pay for towering cathedrals and to support men in high places. To lift up the message of Scripture concerning God's graciousness, Luther set forth his distinction between the demands in God's Word and the grace God freely gives to us. The first was designated "law" and the second "gospel." Taking a cue from Paul, Luther taught that the law, or the Ten Commandments, produced an awareness of sin and guilt, whereas the gospel, seen in the teachings, death, and resurrection of Jesus, revealed God's free and unmerited forgiveness.[1]

The Reformation had the potential for reducing the separation. However, for various reasons, "law" for Luther took on additional dimensions, and thus he unwittingly encouraged the separation. One of these dimensions had a theological look. "Law" was associated with the "left hand of God" and with such people as police and parents. Since there were only two major groups of people—the peasantry and the aristocracy or the working class and the ruling class—the need for law and order was intense. Unrest was rampant. Indeed, there was an underlying fear of chaos and lawlessness in Luther's concept of the "left hand of God," and when he spoke of a "kingdom on the left," princes and dukes also received theological sanction in the law-enforcement system. The process of creating distance from those who comprise the workforce was set in motion.

Actually, what Luther had on his left hand was a powder keg, and in 1525 it exploded in the Peasants' War. For nearly a century it had been smoldering among the peasant farmers who made up most of the workforce. However, because of heavy taxes, restriction on membership in the trade guilds, and discounts for the clergy, the lid blew off the unrest. Even the struggling merchants and shopkeepers joined in. With the base of support broadened to include people in towns as well as folks in the country, the fires soon spread out of control. When Luther preached about the freedom of the Christian, he had a purely religious meaning in mind, but to the people who stood and listened to his sermons (there were no pews in those days) the liberating sound of the gospel went much further. Quite understandably, the people applied it to their own weekday lives and their daily-work concerns.

History confirms that there were economic grievances. Justice for the masses was needed. However, Luther feared such an emphasis would cause people to lose sight of God's grace. His blindspot was the fact that he did not see the connection between the two. Roland Bainton wrote that Thomas Müntzer, the "revolutionary saint," had "insight to see what no one else in his generation observed, that faith itself does not thrive on physical exhaustion." He then quoted from Müntzer, "Men whose every moment is consumed in the making of a living have no time to learn to read the Word of God."[2] Müntzer was in touch with what Abraham Maslow in our century described as the "hierarchy of needs." Before a person can take on the search for faith or meaning in life, his or her physical needs must be adequately met.[3]

Thus, unfortunately but understandably, Luther supported the emperor, princes, and police to put down the peasants' revolt, although his own preaching had fueled the very fires these authorities sought to extinguish.

There was one other factor that led to the separation between church and daily work in the sixteenth and subsequent centuries. In the minds of most people, the "right hand of God," the gospel, and the "kingdom on the right" became embodied in the church and in the clergy who personified the church.

There was more than anthropomorphic phrasing involved in the concepts of God's left and right hands. There was more than a difference in emphasis. There was a difference in kind, in other words, genuine separation. To say that the difference was merely one of degree is to do an injustice to both words and history.

Civil authorities in the kingdom on the left, including jailers and executioners, did not have to be Christians. Through them God exercised the left hand of wrath and preserved external peace whether the people knew it or not. In the kingdom on the right, however, Christian faith and awareness were all-important. Indeed, in this kingdom God personally ruled and dwelled.[4] Thus, we may read of God's incognito activity in the weekday world,[5] but in the church we have God's "Real Presence."[6]

Moreover, when Paul wrote that the gospel not only was new compared with the law but also was of greater glory than the law, it was an open invitation for the clergy, as caretakers of the gospel, to emerge from the Reformation on a higher plateau than the laity. To this day when someone says, "I'm just a layman," the meaning is "I'm not well informed." Ironically, the better versed the clergy become in the Bible and theology, the further from the laity and the weekday work world they move. And on Sunday when the two "kingdoms" assemble for worship, the difference or separation in many churches is, to this day, accentuated by what they wear. The clergy are set apart by dress as well as by title. Some lay persons may speak of God's presence with them in daily life, but their experience does not hold a candle—literally—to God's presence in church, which is symbolized in the robes, surplices, stoles, and liturgical headgear worn by pastors, bishops, cardinals, and popes. The difference is so visible that what takes place in church on Sunday seems unreal compared to what happens at work during the week. Clothes may not make one a pastor or priest, but they do make one a man or woman of "the cloth".

Although it might seem that in post-Reformation days these two "kingdoms" were divided against themselves, they were not really, for in practice they were united against the material needs of the people, one by spiritualizing God's care, the other by protecting the status quo and the privileges of the ruling class.

The Religion of the Industrial Revolution

The Protestant faith, even though it was not established everywhere, was the unofficial religion of the first Industrial Revolution. If this statement tends to leave Roman Catholic readers feeling left out, what William Ophuls says makes many Protestants unhappy. The Protestant faith, he wrote, provided "justification for acquisitiveness and other bourgeois traits."[7] It isn't just the tone but the content that is offensive.

Ophuls was talking about the Protestant work ethic, a frame of mind that rowed ashore with the Pilgrims when they landed at Plymouth. One century before Ben Franklin discovered electricity at the end of a kite string and two centuries before technology translated that discovery into power-driven machines, the Puritans, under the influence of John Calvin, held a belief that did as much to join church and daily work—though in a distorted way—as Luther's doctrine of two kingdoms did to separate them.

The Puritans were not afraid of hard work. They saw it as a defense against all the temptations that led to an unclean life. Waste of time was the first and, in principle, the deadliest sin. "The most trifling actions that affect a man's credit are to be regarded," Franklin once said.

> The sound of your hammer at five in the morning, or nine at night, heard by a creditor, makes him easy six months longer; but, if he sees you at a billiard-table, or hears your voice at a tavern, when you should be at work, he sends for his money the next day; demands it, before he can receive it, in a lump.[8]

The interesting thing about this quote is that Ben was a Deist, not a Puritan; he lived in Philadelphia, not Massachusetts, and in 1776, not 1650. The work ethic was making its presence felt in the new world.

As we know, religious faith was important to the Puritans; the desire to express it freely was one reason they came to these shores. And no aspect of their faith did more to join grace to the workplace—pseudo grace, that is—than the doctrine of predestination. How this happened is a cornerstone in early American history, one that is rarely noticed or acknowledged.

To understand how this occurred, all one has to do is to imagine what it was like for Peter and Mary Puritan to hear the Rev. Jonathan Edwards thunder from the pulpit that God elected some folks to be the recipients of eternal salvation and others to be fuel for the fires of hell. It did not take too many sermons like this before the folks in the pews began to look for some sign, some assurance, that they were among the saved rather than among the damned.

Being in church twice on Sunday was not enough. They had to live through the days in between with the preacher's words ringing in their ears. Thus it was that during the week signs showed up that related to weekday work. One sign was the accumulation of material goods; the other was the desire to work hard to obtain them. Both of these signs became proof positive that a person was standing in the fullness of God's grace and was visibly blessed by God.[9]

Looking back, we could reasonably assert that religious faith provided a powerful incentive to work hard. The more material goods one succeeded in obtaining the more proof one had that he or she had been elected for eternal salvation. However, to keep the hard work from calling attention to what the believer had accomplished on his or her own, the desire to work hard was seen as a sign of election. Unfortunately, this put divine favoritism just around the mental corner. God must have had a reason for electing some and not others, and that reason had to be found in what they were doing. With monetary success came the feeling that they must be doing something right.

The Calvinist doctrine of predestination did not start out in relation to the workplace. It began as a way of attributing all glory and freedom to God. However, in his illuminating work *The Protestant Ethic and the Spirit of Capitalism*, Max Weber observes that theologians often have in mind an idea quite different from the one that finds its way into the daily lives of people.[10] The beliefs that survive do so because they work, they serve some purpose; indeed, the furthest thing from Calvin's mind was to provide sanction for prosperity.

Yet, sanction is what he provided. Making money, so long as it was done legally, became so important that the opportunity to turn a profit was considered God's "call."[11] To choose a less gainful way to function was a denial of one's calling and a refusal to be God's steward. Thus, the pursuit of wealth came to be viewed as a duty. Not only was it morally permissable, but it also carried with it a divine mandate.

Perceptive lay persons found support in their views from a Puritan writer and preacher by the name of Richard Baxter. He helped relate the Puritan understanding of grace to daily work when he explained God's invisibility with an analogy from the marketplace. Weber describes Baxter's analogy: "Just as one can carry on profitable trade with an invisible foreigner through correspondence, so is it possible by means of holy commerce with an invisible God to get possession of the one priceless pearl." Then Weber notes that "these commercial similes . . . are thoroughly characteristic of Puritanism, which in effect makes man buy his own salvation."[12]

The transaction no longer took place in church or through the mediation of priests as in the sixteenth century. Through the work ethic people had found a way of dealing with a God who was believed to have sorted out the human merchandise, marking some for "sending" and others for "receiving."

In a widely publicized study it was found that four out of every five people tested believe that America offers an opportunity for financial security to all who are willing to work hard.[13] So widespread is this belief that writers of this 1981 study call it the "American work ethic" rather than the "Protestant work ethic." However, evidence will be shared in the next chapter which suggests that the religious connections to this work ethic are still very much alive, at least among mainline church members. The work ethic may indeed be tied in with being American, but the fact remains that while we may be Lutherans, Baptists, Roman Catholics, or otherwise on Sunday, we are all Calvinists on Monday, successful or disillusioned.

A Model for Management/Labor Relations

Few would deny that when we take a deep breath in our economic world, we inhale some of Adam Smith's thought.[14] However, both Calvin and Luther, through their views on callings and stewardship, also provided some of the air we breathe. Although the modern results were not intended by Luther and Calvin, their views are influences in the separation between labor and management which we know today.

When the sixteenth century dawned, the notion that spiritual power was above temporal power was already well in force. It was fixed in the minds of laity and clergy alike. The church had led the way in this kind of thinking for centuries with its teaching that the priest was endowed at ordination with an incorruptible character so that the offering of the body and blood of Christ to God in the Mass could be made by a worthy person. Luther made a valiant attempt to remove this separation of powers in two ways.

One was his doctrine of the priesthood of believers, whereby all Christians are "priests" through baptism. In this concept rank was eliminated. Priests were born, not made—born of the Spirit. To say that ordination made one a priest was to deny that he was a priest through baptism.[15] However, when Lutheran clergy were ordained to "rightly proclaim the Word and rightly administer the Sacraments," the priesthood-of-believers concept was pushed into the background, where it remains to this day.

The other thing Luther did was to teach that all worthwhile work is a calling from God. He perceived God to be tailor, shoemaker, and cook, as well as prince and preacher. Those whose work was regarded as lowly he held up in high esteem as doing God's work, even if the work was that of a milkmaid or one who hauled manure.[16] Thus, everyone whose work made a contribution to society was thereby doing God's will. Apparently, however, Luther had more esteem for the offices of shoemaker or milkmaid than for the spiritual potential of the persons who held these offices. "The world and the masses are and always will be un-Christian," he wrote, "even if they are baptized and Christian in name."[17] This perspective emerged in the Peasants' War and has at least contributed to the climate out of which management's view of labor developed in our own country.

No sooner had all Christians been identified as "priests" and elevated in name than new distinctions began to emerge. The ordained Protestant was called a "pastor," whereas no one else in the congregation had that title. Luther tried to safeguard separation by referring to the pastor's calling as a function. However, with the location and time for the proclamation of the gospel being in church on Sunday, and the location and time for the fulfilling of the law being at work on Monday, it was not long before the pastor's function assumed the nature of a prerogative. Thus, when he stepped into the pulpit he entered an "office" also, and performing the sacraments was something the laity did only in an emergency.

The concept of everyone's work being a calling had the unintended effect of locking everyone in place, both the privileged and unprivileged. When someone's work is regarded as a calling from God, it is set in holy cement. Thus, one can see how the separation between workers with brains and those specializing in brawn could come to be seen as divinely inspired.

Over the centuries there has developed an unwritten caste system in the way various kinds of work and workers are viewed. Clergy persons are "called," ordained of God. Teachers, doctors, and lawyers are more often thought of as professional persons, or those with a vocation. The term "occupation" seems to fit merchants, musicians, or funeral directors, whereas society is more comfortable referring to carpenters, machinists, and brick layers as having a trade. In our efforts to alter these images, we need to refer to them candidly so that what is new can have some point of relevant comparison.

The concept of callings also attributed a high degree of accountability or stewardship to one's work. If we work because God works, then to stop working or to shirk one's duty is to fail God as well as one's colleagues or employers. Actually, we have two employers, One who is almighty and one who has more limited powers. Weber writes that in the Reformation one thing was "unquestionably new." The fulfillment of one's duty in daily work was "the highest form [of] moral activity . . . the individual could assume."[18] This gave everyday work a religious significance, but it was one laced with law more than gospel. Should one have been laid off, as often happens today, the law did not stop working. Indeed, the law never seemed to know when to quit.

With this kind of thinking in force through the church from century to century, the stage was set for Frederick Winslow Taylor, the father of "scientific managment" or what is more popularly known as "time and motion study."

It was Taylor's belief that every component of a job could be timed and measured in order to come up with the one best way to get it done. The historic test case occured at the Bethlehem Iron Works in Pennsylvania around 1910 where 80,000 tons of ninety-two-pound iron "pigs" had to be moved. Each piece of iron had to be lifted from a pile, carried up an inclined plank, and dumped into a waiting railroad car. After watching the men for a few days Taylor concluded that a first-class handler could carry forty-seven tons a day instead of the average twelve. After Taylor had performed the "time and motion" study, the next step was to offer the men a 60 percent increase in wages if they performed the job and then weed out those who could not do it.[19] That was stewardship being practiced in the workplace—offering the highest wages to those whose abilities and effort could earn them.

Taylor further decided that people with the most intelligence, skill, and lasting devotion to the company should be the managers. Their power would not lie in brute strength but in their scientifically determined command of the details and specifications of work itself. It was assumed that everyone on the shop floor would benefit from the division between brains and brawn, thought and action. Thus, in this century the premise that the workplace should be completely divided between order-givers and order-takers has been established.[20]

The "calling" dimension surfaced when Taylor further declared that precise definitions of the job were not only management's prerogative but also its "sacred duty." He had an engineer's faith that technology defined the nature of the job; human beings were secondary. "In the past, man has been first; in the future the system must be first."[21] Actually, an economic system had been in force from the earliest days of the Industrial Revolution. In it some men were first, and other men, women, and children were second, third, and fourth.

The ultimate irony came in 1921 when Lenin, fresh from the success of the Russian Revolution, saw Taylorism as a "combination of the refined brutality of bourgeois exploitation and a number of the greatest scientific achievements in the field of analysing mechanical motions. . . ." The communist leader then observed, "We must organise in Russia the study and teaching of the Taylor system and systematically try it out and adapt it to our own ends."[22] Thus, we have the ironic situation in which on military and political fronts our nation has in recent years shown a determination to contain Soviet-style communism at all costs, but on the economic level the two nations are both doing the same thing. In the name of production quotas we serve the same economic god. Although this god is called the "state" in one country and the "system" in the other, in both places the managerial chief priests give the orders and the laboring laity carry them out.

The Carpenter's Education

It would be more historically accurate to say that the subject matter of this book has been on the way for nearly two thousand years. The spirit that has animated the content began, not in a theological-school classroom, but in the humble home of a first-century carpenter, who lived there with his wife and several children, the oldest of whom was named Jesus.

We assume that for much of thirty years Jesus worked at the carpenter's trade alongside Joseph. At some point he may have become the main bread winner of the family. His religious education was an interaction between his own thoughts, the teachings of the Old Testament and the religious authorities, and the understanding of the people of his day. He locked horns with the authorities but was well received among ordinary people. His experience as a carpenter and his link with God contributed to both results.

Mark wrote that "the common people heard him gladly (Mark 12:37, KJV)."[23] Although the word "common" has a denigrating sound—like "rank and file"—this short sentence casts a long shadow into the twentieth century, eighth decade. Mark placed it in the context of Jesus' critique of the scribes, who liked to "go about in long robes, and to have salutations in the market places and the best seats in the synagogues . . . and for a pretense make long prayers" (Mark 12:38-40).

Jesus touched something deep in lay people, which might have enabled them meaningfully to identify with his words. The inferiority they felt in relation to religious authorities was not a pleasant feeling. It did not reinforce faith. But here was a man on their side who spoke with an authority of his own. He was looking at religion and life from their point of view. While there was no sign of open conflict, the people may have had plenty to say among themselves in the privacy of their homes, especially after hearing Jesus speak.

In pedagogical but practical terms, serving the woodworking needs of folks in and around Nazareth was an experience that let Jesus get to know the language and lifestyle of the people.

Later he employed the vocabulary of the people to share the thoughts about God and society that had taken shape in his mind.

It was probably because of his close contact with working people that Jesus first selected fishermen and carpenters to be among his followers. The movement known as Christianity and the institution that evolved from it called "the church" began among unlettered persons, those whose "major" had been in the school of life.

The thinking of Jesus broke through patterns of thought that had developed over the centuries. Some of these ideas were present in the Old Testament. Some were new with him. Jesus was the breakthrough. News of the breakthrough has continued throughout history, and in the Reformation of the sixteenth century it received a fresh start. However, relating that news to the thought patterns of people in their daily work has not been a part of the story. We have not pursued theology with the people's workplace in mind. Thus, in order to make faith fit the empirical world, most lay persons have made an accommodation of their own, as we shall see in the next chapter.

Conversation Starters

Faith does not thrive on physical exhaustion. Do you agree or disagree? Why?

What a minister or priest wears in church makes it easier to feel God's presence there. Do you agree or disagree? Why?

Pseudo grace in relation to daily work is better than no grace at all. Do you agree or disagree? Why?

To say that ordination makes one a priest is to deny that one is already a priest through baptism. Do you agree or disagree? Why?

How does the idea that one's work is a calling relate to the present tendency to engage in different kinds of work during one's life?

The division between order-givers and order-takers is divinely ordained. Do you agree or disagree? Why?

Why is the gap between Sunday and Monday hard for some to acknowledge?

As long as a subject is never discussed it doesn't really exist. Do you agree or disagree? Why?

Chapter 2

The Operational Faith
of the Laity

The reality of the Protestant or American work ethic is no secret. Surveys are taken every so often to test its pulse to make sure that the spirit of capitalism is alive and well. What seems to get the silent treatment in such surveys, however, is the influence of the work ethic on the religious faith of people. Even more surprising is that lay people are often told in religious study materials that faith has an impact on daily work, or should. Sometimes the materials call for a verbal witness, and sometimes they exhort persons to be ethical and honest in business. What is never mentioned is the part that the Protestant work ethic already plays or the impact of the workplace on the faith of lay persons. In any event the outcome is that a concept of pseudo grace is operating in the workplace. And pseudo grace is not grace. It is the opposite of grace, as I shall try to make clear in this chapter and the next. Whether a person's exposure to God's unmerited grace one hour a week in church will be able to influence his or her attitude towards daily work when a distorted version already occupies that territory is open to question.

What makes the influence of this work ethic even more serious is its pervasive nature. It can safely be assumed or asserted that the faith of all people is affected by it. Exploring the anatomy of the work ethic among church folk anywhere is a reflection of that anatomy everywhere in the religious community. The interest of Judson Press in publishing this book testifies to the ecumenical nature of the subject matter. As noted in the Preface, in case you skipped it, we may be Baptists, Lutherans, Roman Catholics, or otherwise on Sunday, but we are all Calvinists on Monday. The Protestant work ethic is that part of the ecumenical movement that belongs to the great unsaid, but it is ubiquitous.

One school of theology on the East Coast may have come close to facing the issue of the work ethic when it devoted fourteen days to "Making the Transition: Seminary to Parish." It was a program for seniors. Thirteen and one-half days were spent on how to maintain one's spiritual life, resolve conflict, manage time and personal finances, do parish evangelism, and use a computer—all worthy subjects. Three hours of one day were given to what was called "Popular Theology in the Parish" or the beliefs of the people.

I do not know whether the Protestant work ethic's influence on the faith of the laity was a part of this three-hour period. It was not mentioned in the title of the session. What was implicit in the title, however, is that the theology of the laity is different from that of seminarians or the clergy. What is also implicit is the origin of lay theology. Lay theology may be in the parish but it is not derived from the ordained leadership. It was brought in from the lay world. It comes from another source.

We observed this other source in chapter 1 in the section on "The Religion of the Industrial Revolution." In this chapter we consider the beliefs that make the work ethic what it is today in our country. What are these beliefs that become operational on Monday and for practical or economic purposes replace the ones to which people are exposed on Sunday (or with which they are mentally familiar)? How does the true meaning of grace become distorted in the work ethic? What part do religious beliefs play in the thinking of Christians and non-Christians who are under the influence of the work ethic during the week?

Some of the answers to these questions come from research conducted among folks in Luther's backyard, as described in the Preface. However, such data is supplemented and confirmed in findings from other sources that will be identified as necessary.

Focus on Creation

When it comes time for the offering, the accent is on God as Creator, the Giver of "our selves, our time, and our possessions."[1] However, the major emphasis in prayers, hymns, and sermons (except for Stewardship Sunday) is on our redemption in Jesus Christ. On Monday, the minor key changes to a major one; creation replaces redemption. Moreover, the emphasis in church on our personal relationship to God—a direct by-product of the Reformation—provides the background for believing that God "personally" distributes the talents. Consequently, as we shall see, divine partiality emerges as the unspoken foundation for daily work's operational faith.

In a question headed "Theology from 8 to 5", the clue search participants selected from four statements any that meaningfully provided a theological backdrop for daily work. Eighty-five percent said that "God has blessed me with certain talents and opportunities," whereas only 8 percent said "God lets the genes determine the distribution of aptitude and capacity."

This study result was confirmed on a Sunday morning when a large sample of worshipers were asked to jot down on the back cover of their morning bulletins what they were thankful for in connection with their daily work. People from more than five thousand congregations participated, and when the open-ended response was analyzed, the first of thirty-six categories— far out in front of other thoughts—was "ability and talents." "God's personal involvement in daily work in the form of guidance and help" showed up in the sixth category, but only 3 percent of the respondents had it on their minds.[2]

Thus, what emerged on top in relation to daily work were talents that the Creator was believed to have given personally, talents that distinguished people as individuals. Belief that God provided guidance in the use of these talents was negligible.

This kind of thinking appears in the words of comedienne Carol Burnett. In an interview she mused:

> I don't know if I'm correct, but I've come to believe that we're all
> dealt a hand in life. God has given us a free will, choices to make,

and how we play our hand is up to each of us. You can be given
a royal flush and still blow it, but if you're pretty good at the game
you'll play it right.[3]

She likens the Creator to a card dealer who distributes the cards
and then leaves us alone to play our hand. It would seem that
if the Dealer doesn't look at what is dealt, we have a genetic
lottery. The Dealer is impartial. On the other hand, if the cards
are selected by the Dealer, we have partiality. Either way, to
follow Carol's thought, what happens next is our move; we have
free will. This thought is fine for those with a good hand but
not really fair or comforting for those who are dealt a poor one.
One's choices very much depend on one's hand.

Perhaps one reason Ms. Burnett is not certain that she is
correct in her belief is that the Declaration of Independence has
had a rather powerful place in our upbringing in America, with
its emphasis on the idea that "all men are created equal." Whether Thomas Jefferson and David Hume (the philosopher from
whom Jefferson borrowed this idea) were aware of leaving out
the female half of the human population is not known. What is
known is that both were well aware of human differences, which
they perceived to be the products of environment, or life after
birth. Adam Smith, the economist who influenced Jefferson,
was known to have written that "the difference between the
most dissimilar characters, between a philospher and a common
street porter, for example, seems to arise not so much from
nature, as from habit, custom, and education."[4]

For religious men like Jefferson and others among the
"founding fathers," believing in the effects of the environment
was a way of preserving their faith in divine impartiality. From
that time until the present, children all across America have
been taught that human beings are "created equal." However,
evidence surfaced in the clue search that not many of their
parents believe it. Seven out of ten indicated that the reason
why opportunities and human responses to those opportunities
vary is that "all people are *not* created with equal talents and
intelligence capacity."

Part of the shift in perspective may be due to a rising awareness of IQ tests and SAT scores. The early Americans did not
have such data. While innate intelligence does seem more linked
to nature than to where one lived as a child, evidence from the

clue search and "Affirmations of Faith" study suggests that the teaching of the church about God as Creator may also have contributed to this realization. This is important because if difference in talent and intelligence are by divine design, then we have a way of explaining why some people answer opportunity's knock and why others do not make it to the door; the Creator bestows his "blessings" on some folks but not upon all. The reason we are not all created equal boils down to divine favoritism.

Rewards for Brains and Brawn

On your way home from work, picture yourself driving through two neighborhoods. One is made up of single-family homes with grass, trees, two-car garages, and space. The other is composed of deteriorating row houses with no grass or trees around them and with cars parked in the street.

Participants in the clue search were asked to indicate what they felt were the reasons for the differences in these two neighborhoods. They revealed clear agreement that the difference had to do with hard work. Upwards of 70 percent identified with the thought that if you want a new house, you have to work for it. Moreover, they agreed that people who work hard are entitled to what they have.

The word "entitled" implies that the worker feels he or she deserves the new house, pleasant neighborhood, and so on. One's home may not be a castle, but it is brick-and-mortar proof of one's labor and effort. An editorial on federal budget cutting ended with these words: "The taxpayers' claim to be entitled to a little more of the national pie is based on a very simple argument: they made their money the old-fashioned way; they earned it."[5] When Geraldine Ferraro accepted her party's history-making vice-presidential nomination, she noted that the promise of America is that if you work hard and play by the rules, you can earn your share of America's blessings. If you think about it, however, when "blessings" are earned, they are not gifts but are rewards to which one is entitled.

However, the word "entitled" or "deserve" in relation to work is a curious one. There are thousands of different kinds of jobs, but there are basically only two kinds of work. One is the kind that is done for its own sake. Attached to it there are no bosses or clocks or profits or wages, and usually it is rewarding in itself. It's more fun than work. The other kind is done in return for a wage or salary—at docks or in factories, offices, schools, or stores where one is a slave to time-keeping, expectations, incentives, procedures, and all kinds of "carrots" that are supposed to help one get through the day. No doubt most readers would agree that the words "entitled" and "deserve" are linked with the second kind of work. The implication is that the more work is truly *work*, the more we feel entitled to a reward or compensation.

Unfortunately, America *is* a tale of two cities. Some folks, perhaps many, work very hard all day but have little to show for it, while others work in air-conditioned places and go home to quiet streets in the suburbs or condos high above the noise of the city. Both groups have hard work as a common denominator, but the results of their hard work are not the same. There is a different value placed on hard work depending upon whether one's work is cerebral or physical. Talents seem to carry more income potential if they relate to the mind rather than to the body—unless, of course, one is a professional athlete or model. The idea that "you can't get anywhere without a college education" reflects this holdover feeling from the past, but today a number of people are discovering that you cannot get very far *with* one either. Nevertheless, behind opportunity and education there is the feeling that those who have a degree have worked for it, and so they deserve a better income.

The God Connection

Not only does God play a part in the work ethic as the giver of talents, but God also has a part to play after the hard work is over. More than half of the participants in the clue search perceived a link between God's favor and their standard of living. The belief persists that faithful use of God-given talents somehow wins material "blessings" or the income to purchase them.

As recently as 1983 this came to light. In a study involving two thousand lay persons and more than eight hundred clergy, more lay respondents agreed than disagreed that God blesses us if we "live right, work hard, and manage well."[6] It is worth noting, though, that clergy respondents were in strong disagreement with this idea, probably because it sounded too much like earning or doing something to win God's favor. It was the opposite of grace.

There appears to be a contemporary interpretation of the Protestant work ethic; God provides the talent, we provide the hard work, and then God adds a reward for faithful service in the use of our talents.

There is a variation to this theme in the fundamentalist churches. For example, in a very fast growing church on the Philadelphia Main Line, there has been an attempt to play down the thought that God rewards hard work. This church says that affluence is the result of a "proper relationship with the Lord." If one accepts Jesus as personal savior, then God responds by providing material "blessings." The pastor has compared it to God selecting the Israelites to demonstrate to a "sinful and fallen world" just what God can do for those who trust wholly in the Lord.[7]

The sound of these words about earning or deserving is heard again, with faith replacing hard work as the salvation winner. Actually, the affluence was there before, not after, the "acceptance of Jesus as personal Savior." Indeed, their affluence is one of the primary reasons that prospective members accept Jesus or join the church, a process which begins with their being invited to a four-course "executive dinner" in a home or at a country club. At this dinner movie stars, professional athletes, or leading business persons give testimonies concerning how much they have been blessed.

Their motive for receiving Christ into their lives is not fear of eternal damnation, a reporter made clear, or some crisis in their lives. It is more likely to be thankfulness, "not for some great ability in myself, but for the abilities we receive through God." Both humility and belief in God as Creator put in an appearance. However, since the awareness of God's part comes after the material things have been accumulated, the "conversion" comes across as a way to justify having received them. The "blessings" that came as a result of trusting God were there in advance, making it much easier for the church to say that God had done God's part and then to accept them as members.

The theme of hard work here is muted. All is of God, causing the reporter to write that "God is alive and well on the Main Line." Such were the words printed on the cover of the *Today* magazine of the *Philadelphia Inquirer*, along with the picture of a woman wearing a fur coat and holding a Bible. Christianity was described as "flourishing" along the Main Line due to a combination of country-club luncheons, fashion shows, and the opportunity to "know Jesus." Stockbrokers and lawyers can attend Bible-study breakfasts before buying the *Wall Street Journal*.

Sadly, affluent believers are not the only ones who see a connection between God and material possessions. A "have not" wrote in response to the question on neighborhood differences: "When I see a beautiful home my thought is that someday I will have a nicer home than I do now. Nice things come to those who wait and trust in God." She had the trust that the Main Line congregation had. What she lacked was the dowry.

The Implication

If material things are rewards for hard work or for belief or if they are signs of being blessed, then lack of such things must mean that God is not pleased with the efforts of some folks or their faith. Poverty implies that the poor either are not working hard enough or do not believe properly. This was implicit in write-in responses to the clue search question on differences in neighborhoods. The concept was not stated in the question but was presumably in the minds of participants who wrote down their thoughts in space provided for such a purpose. The poor were described as "lazy, ungodly, or undeserving." One person wrote: "Just because some cannot obtain better housing does not make illegitimate the housing that others have successfully earned with hard work, nor does it necessarily obligate them to alleviate the situation."

This person's statement does not explicitly say that the poor are lazy, but it is implicit in the words "that others have successfully earned with hard work." Beth Hess, professor of sociology, draws the following conclusion from data from the U.S. Census and the 1980 elections. Her words articulate the attitude or spirit implicit in the common stereotype that the poor are lazy, when she writes:

The "Protestant work ethic" still informs our attitudes, so that those who succeed are considered virtuous, while those who fail are flawed. Above all, people still believe that it is the individual who is responsible for his or her own condition. If poverty can be attributed to irresponsible sexual behavior, poor work habits, or an inability to keep a marriage together, then is it not unfair to ask other people—hardworking, abstemious, conscientious spouses— to pay for these mistakes?

Survey data, as well as the 1980 election returns, suggest that most Americans attribute poverty to the shortcomings of individuals, and see themselves as unfairly taxed in order to support people whose behavior is repugnant. Sinners must be punished— by being unable to enjoy that for which others work so hard.[8]

To put this in theological terms, predestination is still with us. It may not divide people up for their eternal destiny, but it does divide people up for their earthly journey. Calvinistic theology has moved away from its heaven-or-hell focus, but its effect on the way many think continues through the work ethic.

There is one other implication. The operational faith that we are describing in this chapter as being active from Monday through Friday in daily work has as its bottom line our economic system. When a pollster like George Gallup reports that most Americans believe in God, he has in effect touched base with the American workplace and the economic priorities that govern it. If one prefers to say that God and our system are tied together, one might put it this way: Belief in God as Creator serves to reinforce what we do during the week and the rewards that come from what we do. It could also be expressed the other way around. The work we do during the week and the rewards that accrue to us because of it, reinforce our belief in God.

The Unintended Harvest

Even the thought of unemployment is devastating to generations conditioned by the Protestant work ethic to regard paid work as the chief end of industrialized humanity. If one believes that hard work brings rewards and that God has given people special talents and has called them to exercise these talents in a certain field of endeavor, for such a "believer" to have the employment rug pulled away is an extremely disillusioning experience. One's faith is being challenged. In a sense these beliefs have become counterproductive. They come back to haunt a person when the situation in life undergoes a shift.

A pastor in Michigan pointed to this when he spoke of church members who lose their jobs and also lose their interest in the church. Instead of being drawn to the church in a time of need, they are repelled. He said: "If you have been indoctrinated to believe that if you work hard God will take care of you, then when unemployment strikes you begin to wonder why God did this or what you did to deserve this."

The work ethic is unable to distinguish reasons for unemployment. Whether lay offs are due to the effect of foreign imports on domestic markets, plant relocations, or automation, the work ethic continues to exercise its tyranny over the believer. Medical research has found a link between the suicide rate and the rise in unemployment. Studies in Britain and North America consistently find that 25 to 50 percent of men of working age were out of work at the time they took their lives.[9]

The work ethic is powerless to introduce the true meaning of grace into the workplace. It, not the poor or unemployed, is flawed. Like the left hand of God it only knows how to reward or punish. It cannot redeem.

"I feel ashamed," said a man laid off when a railway shop closed down. "I go round the back streets and I don't want to meet people. They say, 'Aren't you in a job yet?' and I feel ashamed. I don't like going out any more. It makes you feel you're no longer a useful member of society."[10]

The unemployment figures may drop a percentage point, giving optimists a cause for joy, but among the unemployed today, unlike ten or even five years ago, there are many more people who not only have white faces but have white collars as well. In one company a host of middle-management persons were told to report to one of the top officials. None of them knew that any of their colleagues had been called also. Upon arrival they discovered a line of friends there ahead of them. One by one they were ushered into the office only to stand briefly before the executive and be told that they were to return to their desks, collect their belongings, and leave the building; their services were terminated. Quite literally they were facing a "firing" line. Finding other employment at the age of fifty is not easy, but the company did not seem to care.

The male segment of society is by no means the only one to

experience disillusionment due to the work ethic. Linda Irving became an assistant buyer for a famous New York department store. She was twenty-two, bright, assertive, and highly motivated to succeed.

"I believed strongly in the Protestant work ethic: work hard and you will be rewarded," she said. But she wasn't. Her white peers were promoted ahead of her. Unhappy and frustrated, Irving resigned after three years and joined an exclusive Washington, D.C., department store as a buyer. There she encountered the same frustrations. She became bitter and hostile, and withdrew from her work and co-workers. She was not surprised—indeed, was somewhat relieved—when she was fired.[11]

For people who have held welfare in disdain all their lives to have to turn to it suddenly to survive or to have to take a job they have considered menial is a humbling experience. White folks who experience this are coming to know what many black folks have known for a long time.

Black males are often found standing on street corners in urban areas. On any given morning a truck will drive up and the driver will ask if anyone wants to work. Not many will make a move toward the truck. The jobs filled by the street-corner men are at the bottom of the employment ladder in every respect, from wage level to prestige. They are hard, dirty, uninteresting, and under paid.[12] Neither the men who perform these jobs nor the society that needs to have these jobs done assesses the jobs as worth doing or worth doing well. Both employees and employers hold the jobs in contempt.

Unemployment does something to one's self-esteem. Better paying jobs for the street-corner men are threatening, not just scarce. Given more responsibility and more pay, they know they will fail and they often proceed to do so, proving they were right about themselves all along. The self-fulfilling prophecy is everywhere. The kind of job they can get—frequently only after fighting for it—steadily lowers their self-confidence and self-esteem until finally, terrified of an opportunity even if one does come along, they stand defeated by their own experience, their belief in their own self-worth destroyed and their fears a confirmed reality.[13]

Silence concerning the truth has helped make America a nation that officially exalts equality in such documents as the

Declaration of Independence. Unofficially, we play the game by other rules, rules that divide people into winners and losers, the meritorious and the undeserving, the superior and the inferior. These rules institutionalize inequality. The Judeo-Christian Scriptures reveal a God who sees us as both sinners and forgiven. We have a tendency to see human circumstances in the world as marks of character.

Conversation Starters

Something can become so much a part of life and faith that it is taken for granted as being normal. Do you agree or disagree? Why?

Why is it easier to live with differences in talent and IQ if they can be assigned to the Creator's hand?

The fact that we are not all created equal reflects divine favoritism. Do you agree or disagree? Why?

The harder we work, the more we can feel we are entitled to rewards or compensation. Do you agree or disagree? Why?

Why does society place more value on mental work than upon physical work?

Many poor people are lazy. Do you agree or disagree? Why?

The belief that many of us Americans have in God is really a belief in what the free enterprise system does for us. Do you agree or disagree? Why?

Believing that God rewards faithfulness or hard work can become a source of disillusionment. Do you agree or disagree? Why?

Society regards some jobs with contempt. What might this do to people who hold them?

Chapter 3

Grace on Sunday, Merit on Monday

A school principal on the West Coast took a year off to do what he called "grunt work," moving boxes of food goods around in a warehouse. He kept a diary of daily experiences. Later, when he examined the contents of his job log, he discovered a pattern emerging with relentless persistence. Warehouse work was filled with human encounters of a competitive kind. Looking out for oneself was the unwritten policy that seemed to go with the territory. On Sunday, on the other hand, the Word in church was love, kindness, peace, and gentleness. We say "Word" because it is God's and it boils down to our looking out for each other just as God looks out for us. God's grace is meant to be shared. For the principal, moving from Sunday to Monday was like entering a war zone where a person had to fight the battle all alone. Sunday was like a temporary truce.

Two Languages

Among the four hundred explorers of the "canyon" between Sunday and Monday (participants in the clue search), there were people who did diverse kinds of work. There were farmers, business persons, nurses, schoolteachers, mechanics, doctors, painters, lawyers, computer operators, and secretaries. Twelve words were placed before them, six from the church and six from daily work. The words were mixed up on the list. The task of the participants was to sort them out on the basis of how often each word is heard in the church and/or the workplace.

Since lay persons had helped select them, it was assumed that the words would be familiar. What we did not know was how familiar. Moreover, we knew from which place the words had originated, but we did not know whether they would remain in the church or the workplace or would cross over. Would church words surface again at work on Monday, and would daily-work words enter the pulpit vocabulary and be picked up in the pews on Sunday? We also did not know whether occupational differences would influence the hearing of the gospel.

The words and the order in which they appeared on the survey list are as follows: competent, earn, truth, efficiency, grace, produce, support, performance, acceptance, justice, achievement, and compassion. When the results were compiled, it was clear that words from church and the workplace tended to be grouped separately, as shown in the following table. (Percents equaled 100 in each separate location, but only the percents for "Heard Often" are reported here.)

	Heard Often	
	In Church	At Work
Grace	96%	4%
Compassion	87	14
Truth	86	23
Acceptance	61	19
Support	59	35
Justice	48	24
Efficiency	7	77
Performance	11	75
Earn	14	74
Produce	7	71
Competent	8	67
Achievement	13	66

The numerical totals for each word were subjected to three

statistical tests—chi square, correlation, and T. The results from each test were extremely significant. It was learned from the chi-square test, for example, that if the question were to be put to several million other persons having the same general background, the direction of the percentages would be the same. (For readers who are familiar with statistics, the chi square was off the chart.) For this to happen, the words had to have been very accurate reflections of the two worlds from which they were selected.

These figures from the survey mean several things. For one, the words used in church on Sunday do not, and under present conditions will not, show up at work on Monday, and vice versa. The Sunday/Monday difference is widespread among church-going middle-class Americans from a variety of occupational groups. We can see two dynamics moving in opposite directions. There are two foundations that govern what happens, and they are incompatible. Business is business and religion is religion.

Another message here is that there are two distinct vocabularies in the memories of lay persons who attend church. They coexist and become known, each in its own location. There is one set of ears for Sunday and another set for Monday, one for church and another for daily work.

Although the participants were not asked to identify their understanding of the words, only their hearing of them, words do have meaning. When we examine that meaning we can further understand why there are two different dynamics going on and why they are incompatible.

Most of the work words suggest the extending of maximum effort in order to achieve a desired end. "Efficiency," for example, has to do with getting the best possible product for the cost involved. "Achievement" is a result brought about by resolve or persistence. Compensation or rewards are conditional upon good performance, upon "producing." The church words, on the other hand, suggest empathy or feeling with someone. They express care and concern. They lift up and sustain unconditionally. Grace is heard on Sunday, and merit is operational on Monday. As John Raines, a Protestant professor at Temple University, observed at the Third Annual Conference on Religion and Labor, "As a nation we are trying to keep two sets of books.

One called capital, the other community. One called profits and the other people."[1]

Two Theologies

Implicit in the two languages are two theologies. A lunchtime conversation in a cafeteria at Bethlehem Steel in Allentown, Pennsylvania, provided unprecedented insight regarding these two theologies. Five supervisors were meeting with their pastor, who was visiting them to get better acquainted with his members where they work. He was listening attentively.

The issue they were discussing had to do with employee performance. They all agreed that employees have different talents and different degrees of motivation. They also agreed that to expect perfect performance would be unrealistic. They got stuck on the question of how much imperfection could be tolerated. Paul felt that he owed it to the company and to the rest of his people to expect a good performance from everyone. Russ took comfort in the parable of the talents, in which the ones who performed well were rewarded and the one who did not perform was punished. (See Matthew 25:14-30.) The parable in which each laborer in a vineyard received the same pay was a problem, even though (or because) the meaning has to do with the generosity of God. (See Matthew 20:1-16.) At this point it is relevant for us to report the conversation verbatim. Bill said,

"Don't we confess an understanding of God which says that [God] loves us based on our relation with him, not on how well we perform . . . ?" All heads nodded in agreement. "So if God treats us this way, don't we have an obligation to treat others in the same manner?"

"We do, at church," Paul quickly replied.

"And in our families," Harvey added.

"But how about those we supervise?" [Bill] pressed.

"Bill, there is *no* way you can run a department based on a mushy kind of love," declared Russ. "You just *know* it! You must evaluate performance and reward or remove people based on how well they do. It's that simple."

"In other words, we confess a theology of grace in the church and a theology of good works in the world?" I asked. There was silence.

Someone said, "Pastor, how do you see it?"[2]

It is reasonable to wonder what was going on during the

silence, for there was much to think about. Were the men wondering why there was such a difference between church and work, or between home and work? Were they confronting this difference between grace on Sunday and merit on Monday for the first time, or had Bill articulated something that they had all dimly perceived before? Perhaps they suddenly realized that the reconcilation of this difference wasn't simple, or that there was something odd or wrong about saying that God's way was "mushy." Perhaps their minds had drawn a blank. At least this was true of the pastor. He continued to listen.

We do know that operational faith factors had surfaced in their choice of words concerning talents, performance, and rewards. We also perceive a kind of certainty emerging here that God's way of relating to us won't work in the marketplace, but one wonders why Russ thinks that "you just *know* it."

So that no reader will think for a moment that the church as an institution is somehow immune to what these lay people from Bethlehem Steel were confronting that day in Allentown, it should be noted at this point that two seminary professors, unbeknown to each other, wrote to tell me how prevalent the struggle between grace and merit is in their respective institutions. Excellent students are rewarded with good grades and generally better opportunities for ministry. One then went on to say, "Though we live and talk a theology of grace, we operate within a system of rewards and punishments that is not unlike that of the world at large."

Performance . . . of What?

That two different vocabularies and theologies should emerge from the separation between the church and weekday work is not surprising. Some would even say this simply amounts to two-kingdom activity. Performance and competence are what should be going on in the world and hearing the Good News of grace is what should be going on in the church.

True, there is nothing wrong with competent performance. It is a reasonable expectation, one that accompanies the qualifications for the work one is hired to do. And there are degrees of competence just as there are degrees of talent that need to be matched to a job. "Round pegs" in "square holes" neither fit nor are happy.

However, one topic that deserves consideration is the amount of time spent in the two kingdoms. When twenty minutes of hearing in church about God's free and unmerited grace is compared with forty hours of performing on the job, not only does one wonder what chance grace has but also one has the right to ask, "Performing what?" One academic theologian from Pennsylvania feels that there is no reason for society to reward anything but performance, but then he added, "Neither is there any reason for only a quantifiable contribution to the economy to be reckoned as performance."

How true! Billed as one of the "hottest intellectuals in Reagonomic Washington," black conservative economist Thomas Sowell was a high school dropout, a former delivery boy who joined the Marines and later graduated from Harvard with honors. He then went on to get his Ph.D. in economics from the University of Chicago. He was one of the "have nots," who worked himself up the hard way. In an interview with a *Washington Post* correspondent, Sowell the conservative acknowledged that "greed has a bad name." He asserted, however, that "when you have a system based on being greedy, things get done, because there are some bucks in it."[3]

When only quantifiable work is viewed as performance, efficiency is carried to the extreme. Gary Bryner, former president of the UAW local at Lordstown, Ohio, told how the Ford Motor Company, at one point, timed how long it took to shoot a screw into a car. They knew how fast the gun turned, how long the screw was, and how deep the hole was. They figured that by saving one second on every worker's effort, they would, over a year, make a million dollars.[4] This was Taylorism once again. It was also the tyranny of law and the performance of greed. Hard work of this kind made America what it is today, a nation where some human beings have tried to turn other human beings into robots.

Clarence Jordan, author of the *Cotton Patch Version* of various New Testament books, retells the story of the rich farmer in the twentieth-century terms. He gives the farmer a well-known name. He calls him Sam . . . Uncle Sam.[5]

Uncle Sam planted corn, cotton, and soy beans in his fields, and he worked very hard at it. Up at the crack of dawn, he worked all day and often late into the night to meet the mortgage on his house and the loans for his equipment, and his cars. On Sunday Uncle Sam went to church.

It wasn't long before Uncle Sam realized that by using soil-bank procedures and labor-saving equipment, he could make his fields more productive. As he implemented these ideas, his barns turned into bulging warehouses. His problem was no longer how to make his fields yield more, but what to do with the harvest or where to store it. There were poor people around, but Uncle Sam did not believe that they deserved what he had worked so hard for. Thus, rather than give his grain to fill hungry bellies, he either stored it in steel bins or paid other farmers not to grow so much, thereby helping to keep prices up.

Uncle Sam became so well off that he decided to go on an extended trip. He went to Florida where he could "recline, dine, wine, and shine." The only catch was that not only had he come to serve the wrong master, but he had become like the master he served. He no longer owned his goods and machines; they owned him. He was in bondage to them.

Performance of . . . Power

Pursuit of power is one thing that underlies Taylor's philosophy of scientific management. Workers are to be quiet yet responsive cogs in the industrial machinery. They are to listen while management tells them what to do. Someone has defined power as the ability to say, "Jump!" and have others ask, "How high?" It is both the carrot that tempts and the stick that drives people up a corporate ladder. Power means being able to ask for advice and not having to take it. Workers are viewed simply as machines that happen to have inconvenient emotional and physical needs. Though many companies have softened the precisely measured, dehumanizing time-study approach to work efficiency, the basic thrust remains.[6]

It is customary for management to blame labor when there is a decline in productivity. However, in a 1983 national study done by pollster Daniel Yankelovich, it was found that managerial practices are out of sync with changing values and attitudes. Of the 845 workers randomly selected from all walks of life, 70 percent were in service-related industries.[7] This dramatic shift from manufacturing fields and assembly lines means that more workers are going to be in the position of utilizing their own judgment on the job. In other words, people are thinking more. They are asking, for example, how the demands of authoritarian management can be squared with the beliefs and practices of a political democracy.

It should be noted here that the church is in no position to point a finger of judgment at the managerial practices of industrial America. As we observed in chapter 1, hierarchical power is a long-standing tradition in the church and the Reformation did little to change it. A few years ago one church body hired Hayes Associates to do a study of each job in its bureaucratic structure. Hayes has been used in many secular places of employment and what seems to follow its assessment is praise by management and curses by labor. Why? Because its premise is that each job has a certain worth to the company. The criteria for determining this worth are never shared with the employees, but somehow those who hire Hayes find the subsequent report very satisfactory. In the case of the church, out went the sixteenth-century insight of Luther that an ordained clergy person's work is a function and in came secular sanction for the notion that the worth of a person's position is of prime importance. The whole idea of status and rank was reinforced so that performance reviews could be conducted by persons from above, but never the other way around. The hierarchical grid assumed the shape of a Christmas tree with a sacred image on top.

The power to make people perform has been important in the American workplace because of the emphasis capitalism places on competition. However, the trouble with competition is that it separates people into winners and losers. For the five-talent folks or for those who exude an air of authority, the competition may be welcomed. They may even thrive on it. But, unlike the golf world, where a handicap may make competition more even, in the business world—where the drive is to be number one—handicaps are inappropriate. One- and two-talent persons compete with five-talent people for the same prize, and so there really isn't much competition. There are only those who succeed and those who fail, plus a constant winnowing process to decide who's who. As the ad says, "*Fortune* tells you who's winning, who's losing, and how they're doing it."

The Truncated Reformation

Exuding the feeling of having just received an insight, a young lady said, "My parents brought me up to believe that I had to earn whatever I got. Do you think this is why it is difficult for me to believe that God freely forgives me?"

We have alluded to the incompatibility of two basic principles or foundations. However, this is not new. The Protestant church came into being over such an incompatibility, one referred to by Paul as the "principle of works," the other as the "principle of faith." (See Romans 3:27-29.) In the sixteenth century it was believed that Christ supplied merit. The principle of works expressed itself when people said prayers, went to Mass, or purchased indulgences (called "spiritual bouquets" today) in order to transfer merit to their own account or to that of a loved one. The principle of faith emerges in the belief that God's grace is unmerited and already freely given to us in Christ.

While it is disconcerting that a form of the principle of works is employed in theological schools to help students understand the principle of faith, it is true that through their study of Scripture Protestant clergy perceive that salvation is by God's free and undeserved grace. Moreover, in 1983 it was announced that some Roman Catholic scholars also believe that salvation is a free gift, one we can neither buy nor earn by what we do. And when this Good News is shared by pastors from pulpits, it is praiseworthy. Indeed, on the basis of this proclamation it has been declared and celebrated that a reformation occurred in the church. And one must admit that it did—in the pulpit.

What brings the reformation to a sobering halt, however, is for us to find that the message is not getting through to the majority of the folks in the pews. It is not being assimilated. The trickle-down theological process runs into a belief that we must earn whatever we receive. And even for those who hear the message on Sunday, on Monday another story is at work. As one couple said, "We can't think of any Monday words to describe what we believe, so we just invite our friends to church to hear the pastor talk." For them the gospel is a message that goes nowhere, at least not to work. We can assimilate only what we can relate to our life and experience. Daily work comprises such a large slice of life that if it isn't related to the message, the message is diverted. It may not even be heard. Indeed, when a worker seeks to relate grace to the workplace, he or she becomes aware of what is incompatible. Thus, rather than ease the burden of sin, the message can remind the hearer of failure. The Good News can become bad news once it leaves the security of the church building.

The first reformation is truncated, cut off. It has not really occurred—even in the church—until what is said on Sunday has become a part of the Monday world in which most church members spend much of their time, unless, of course, we think of the "church" as comprised only of clergy.

That the reformation is beginning to take hold in the workplace is the subject matter of the second half of this book. However, since for most folks it has not happened yet, we must not lose sight of the fact that until the Good News of God's grace does become a part of the workplace during the week, many church members continue to be under the tyranny of laws and thus separated from God. For most weekday purposes they are not much better off than before the sixteenth-century Reformation occurred. Nowhere did this idea emerge more clearly than in the response of lay persons to several questions in the clue search when the respondents tried to bridge the Sunday/Monday gap. For example, they agreed that competition does not have divine sanction. They do not see the law of the jungle, whether it be in the tropics or in Times Square, as God's will for creation. Moreover, a segment of the participants have an underlying fear, of which they are conscious, that the basic tenets of Christianity are incompatible with a survival-of-the-fittest mentality.

Because by sharing in the study the participants could have become aware of some of the issues for the first time, the last question in the survey encouraged them to back up a bit. It invited them to read over eight thoughts on daily work's relation to God and to indicate those that had occurred to them for the first time because of the study and those that had been on their minds before they had ever laid eyes on it.

The thought that drew the largest response had to do with whether God would forgive a person who had made the increasing of profits a lifelong pursuit. Although this is an idea the pulpit shies away from, 78 percent of those surveyed said that this was an old question, one that had occurred to them before. Seven out of ten said that prior to the study they had even been pondering whether affluence is a sign of God's favor or evidence of human greed.

It is clear from those who identified these as "old questions" that a sense of sin is embedded in our economic system. In a meritocracy such as ours, we can feel guilt whether we fail or succeed. If we lose our shirt, we have not measured up to the system. If we make a bundle, it can be at the expense of the person whose shirt was lost. However, inasmuch as our system is based on greed, as Thomas Sowell said, this is no wonder.

If this concept has a bearing on our relationship to God and perhaps even on our faith awareness of God at work, this should not surprise us. It isn't that God is angry with us or must be seen as a tyrant before grace can be meaningful. It's that sin, whatever its source, distorts our image of God. We hear law on Sunday because the laws of the marketplace are still ringing in our ears. God's grace has been revealed in Christ and when grace changes the way we do business and trade, God won't seem so far away.

The Cross and the Workplace

"Your disks may go to hell, but now your software can be saved." These words appeared in an ad for a machine called "The Savior." The use of biblical language or religious imagery to sell things in the business world is a comparatively new phenomenon. However, the opposite tack—the use of marketplace language to convey biblical meaning—has a long history.

We find the latter occurring when Christians explain what they believe about God's relation to Jesus' death on the cross or what Jesus had in mind when he said, "It is finished!" When we asked the Sunday/Monday explorers what they thought Jesus meant, the most frequently selected response was that he had fully paid the penalty for our sins.[8]

In the history of economic transaction it is axiomatic that somebody must pay and, of course, someone must receive the payment in order for a transaction to occur. In economics we are talking, not just about a concept, but about something happening between people. To many folks justice demands that we only receive what we or somebody else has paid for. There is no such thing as a free lunch. That way work can be duly rewarded. In the marketplace the "penalty" is the price for the commodity being purchased. The price is set by the employer or the company and reflects the supply and demand.

The word "paid" when related to the cross reflects the marketplace and the dynamic of a work-ethic transaction. Salvation becomes the product in this case, and the price is set by the One sinned against, namely God. The price is death. Such is the "wages of sin" which justice demands (Romans 6:23). What attracts some people to Jesus as "personal savior" is that he paid the bill on our behalf; the merits of Jesus have been transferred to our account. For this, they believe, he deserves our eternal praise.

The important factor here is often left unsaid. It is that Jesus paid the bill to God. God was thereby satisfied and for the sake of Jesus lets us off the hook. Actually, this "theory" of the atonement of what happened on the cross did not cost God much at all. In fact, God was the One who was paid. It was a transaction between God and Jesus.

A genuine cost to God is seen in the view expressed in the response "God's desire to take our sin upon himself could be no clearer," chosen by a number of the respondents.[9] Some might say God is taking on our sin in the transaction between God and Jesus, but the reality is blurred by the marketplace language. On the other hand, when the words say that God was the initiator, that Jesus was the human vehicle through whom God revealed grace and forgiveness on the cross, the cost goes sky high. In the first option, God transfers our guilt to Jesus. In the second, God takes our guilt. In the first, God has to get over something within before we feel God's compassion; in the second response, the cross reveals God's compassionate grace from the beginning. In the first, God offers Jesus as our substitute. In the second, God offers himself.

In the first option, theoretically the grace given to us is earned, merited, or deserved by Jesus for his good work on our behalf. In the second, grace is a gift all the way from the One at the top of the tree, God. The idea of earning, deserving, or meriting is not a part of it. Our response to God is gratitude, not for talents received, but for grace alone.

In relation to the theme of this book, the most engaging difference is the way the two perceptions relate to the workplace. In the first option, purchase-oriented commercial language is employed, and the faith it generates keeps faith focused narrowly on Jesus as personal Savior. In the second response, payment language does not appear. The wideness of God's mercy is not thereby restricted. When faith is laden with somebody having earned something or paid for it, there is no room for seeing grace at work within that society's economic system. Such a faith is supported by and indebted to that economic system. On the other hand, when faith is free from ties with our economic system or the concept of transaction, then grace, patience, and understanding become unconditional. They can flow from God to all of God's children; through Jesus all people are drawn to God.

Conversation Starters

We should expect to hear about grace in church and merit at work. Do you agree or disagree? Why?

Business is business and religion is religion. Do you agree or disagree? Why?

What does it mean for the Christian faith if God's grace is thought of as a "mushy kind of love"?

Authoritarian management is an inconsistency in a country that claims to be a democracy. Do you agree or disagree? Why?

To use the principle of works to teach the principle of faith is a contradiction. Do you agree or disagree? Why?

A reformation has not really occurred if it affects what happens on Sunday but not what happens on Monday. Do you agree or disagree? Why?

Is affluence a sign of God's favor or evidence of human greed?

What happened on the cross has no connection with what happens in the marketplace. Do you agree or disagree? Why?

Chapter 4

Work Outside
the Garden of Eden

Although Jesus Christ redeems the situation, the opening pages of Genesis do not exactly strike an upbeat note when it comes to God's link with daily work. Before the story of the Fall there is a mini-acknowledgement of the place of work in human life; the second creation account says that God placed Adam in the garden to "till and keep it." (See Genesis 2:15.) However, it is almost a passing reference and is very much overshadowed by the expulsion of Adam and Eve from Eden after the Fall. It is from this latter part of the story that daily work has received a negative, burdensome image.

A *Time* magazine essay on work borrows from this part of the story; it begins with the words "When God foreclosed on Eden, he condemned Adam and Eve to go to work." Not satisfied with this biblical commentary, the essay goes on to say:

> Work has never recovered from that humiliation. From the beginning, the Lord's word said that work was something bad: a punishment, the great stone of mortality and toil laid upon a human spirit that might otherwise soar in the infinite, weightless playfulness of grace.[1]

The essay writer's thought—that work is bad simply because

God has declared it to be so—overlooks the part that genuine work would play in maintaining the garden. It also seems to overlook the part that human sin played in the expulsion from Eden. The story suggests that God acted in response to what Adam and Eve had done. It was not something God arbitrarily decided to do. Nonetheless, it cannot be denied that for some workers daily work seems to be a curse. "I work in a factory," one man said. "For eight hours a day, five days a week, I'm the exception to the rule that life cannot exist in a vacuum. Work to me is a void and I begrudge every precious minute of my time that it takes."[2] An assembly-line worker in a tractor factory made this comment: "If you didn't dream at work, it would send you mad. It isn't the actual work that kills you in a factory. It's the *repetition.* . . . A man isn't just born to be a worker, like the bees, and nothing else."[3]

The Genesis story's accent on original sin would suggest that we are born for this. Indeed, many a person gets to the nitty-gritty in his or her daily work and feels that there may be some truth in the biblical story of the Fall, that work is some kind of weight placed on the human spirit. And if the nitty-gritty doesn't get to us, there is always Murphy's Law, the seeming inevitability that if something can go wrong, it will.

New Light on an Old Story

Perhaps it is relevant to take a better look at the story in Genesis that has laid the "stone of mortality" upon us. When we do we quickly discover that if we interpret the story literally, the only kind of work that carries the stigma of the expulsion from Eden is farming. While no one would have expected Adam to have any other occupation at that point in prehistoric time, it is soil tilling that is cursed. It is the effort to make the soil productive that is undermined by divine decree. As the text clearly states:

> "Because of what you have done, the ground will be under a curse. You will have to work hard all your life to make it produce enough food for you. It will produce weeds and thorns, and you will have to eat wild plants. You will have to work hard and sweat to make the soil produce anything . . ." (Genesis 3:17b-19, TEV).

Literally speaking, to move from a garden in the Middle East to the steel mills of America or the diamond mines of South Africa or the fabric shops of Hong Kong is to go beyond the limits set by the biblical story, both geographically and occupationally. Moreover, if cursing the ground was God's will, then the agricultural inventions that emerged as by-products of the Industrial Revolution and this century's "Green Revolution" are all successful efforts to circumvent or countermand a divine edict; God's will was to make work harder not easier. As to God's mandate to eat wild plants, Americans don't do that. The response to such a mandate suggests that the local supermarket industry is greater in its corporate strength than is the Almighty.

On the other hand, if one were to abandon the literal interpretation of the Genesis passage and look for something more symbolic, it might be found in the nature of the punishment for original sin. No matter how hard Adam worked to make the earth bear fruit, his efforts encountered frustration; God's law not Murphy's. Thus, from the beginning of the biblical story the appearance of something in opposition to the Protestant work ethic emerges. Rather than declaring that hard work will pay off, the Bible begins on a less promising note.

Moreover, a point that is seldom if ever considered but that is surely worthy of consideration is that the model for weekly labor is established in Genesis 1, prior to the Garden of Eden story in Genesis 2 and 3. The Creator puts in a six-day work week and then is exhausted and takes a day off. Before the Fall and its consequences, the First Worker had already experienced the results of hard work. Thus, before work was saddled with counterproductivity, it was already heavily laden with the experience of fatigue. It isn't just frustration that makes work toilsome. It is also the drain of energy being expended.

Were one to go along with the literalism of the Genesis story, one might say that fashioning the sun and moon and creating the earth out of nothing or out of chaos could even place a strain on the stamina of a Being with infinite power. However, from the vantage point of twentieth century hindsight, the whole idea of saying the Creator either "works" or "rests" is problematical. The terms are too human, too finite to fit one with power to create not just one universe but many, with the possibility of continuous expansion. Besides, the psalmist speaks of God neither resting nor sleeping. (See Psalm 121:3-4.) Nevertheless, when we take into account the world view of the early Hebrews, we must note the distinction in the biblical story between the toll work takes on a worker's body, mind, and spirit, and the way even our best efforts seem to turn sour eventually. In real life these experiences—fatigue and frustration—can overlap. In Genesis they are sequential, distinguishable.

One cannot help but wonder if both of these Genesis stories were after the fact rather than after the Fall; that is, they provided people with plausible explanations for why they were finding work so hard. That the stories surfaced in the literary tradition of a people implies that they may have had a long history and were selected for a purpose. In other words, the stories we have in Genesis 1 through 3 may have been as much a product of the needs of people at that time as they are a divine revelation of the creation of the world and its first inhabitants, and probably much more so.

The perspective this provides is that the frustration experienced in daily work may not have any connection with the will of God in any century. Sin may still be at work, but the kind of punishment for it that Genesis tells about is suspect. God's will as we know it in Jesus is more apparent in the effort to make work less toilsome, not more, less frustrating, not more. Weeds and boll weevils are public nusiances, but they need not be seen as the work of a Creator who wants to make our lives miserable. If grace tells anything about God it is that even God's judgment is tempered with mercy and that retribution is not a hallmark of the Lord's nature. As Jesus noted when telling the story about the weeds that cropped up in the field, "An enemy has done this." (See Matthew 13:28.) God is not that enemy, despite things that can happen that might lead us to think otherwise.

Meaning in Daily Work

One of the more exalted purposes given for daily work is that it is designed to contribute meaning to life. Not only does this completely by-pass the Garden of Eden story, but it also seems more apropos to certain kinds of work. For example, it hardly reflects the sentiment of the person who said:

> People who speak grandiosely of the "meaning of work" should spend a year or two in a factory. The modern worker neither gives

anything to work nor expects anything (apart from his wages) from it. Work, at the factory level, has no inherent value. The worker's one interest is his pay-packet.[4]

Margaret Kane has helped bridge the gap between contemporary theology and industry in Great Britain. She puts her finger on what might be a key discovery: "There are people who having been released from monotonous and pointless work are now discovering themselves for the first time . . . in unemployment."[5]

An unemployed shipyard worker confirmed Kane's observation when he said:

> It's nonsense to say you miss your work when you're paid-off. It all depends on what you've been doing. For over twenty years I worked in the yard as a red-leader. Day in, day out, nothing but dirt and fumes and noise. Home every night covered with paint and grime. Do you really think I miss all that?
>
> For the first time in my life I can really do what I want to do—get on with my gardening and win prizes at the local club with my roses. And I've a lot more time to give to the wife and the grandchildren. Time doesn't hang on my hands—there's the union, the meals on wheels and help at the local church.[6]

Lest anyone think that meaningfulness in daily work is only something that factory and shipyard workers find hard to come by, I would like to mention a dimension that affects many more people. I'm thinking of the high incidence of profanity at work and what this does to workers who happen to be church goers. To my knowledge the information gathered here is unprecedented. The options and percent of response from lay persons to a question concerning profanity at work is presented in rank order as follows:

I see it simply as a habit and not intended to be disrespectful.	53%
It is frustrating to hear a name used thoughtlessly in one place that is used meaningfully in another.	40
I suffer in silence most of the time.	36
Hearing it is like being bombarded by unbelief.	19
No one misuses the Lord's name where I work.	14
When I hear profanity it is an opportunity to bear witness to my faith.	11
There may be some meaning in cursing, but I'm not sure what it is.	11

While a small number said that no one misuses God's name where they work, an even smaller number respond to it with a witness to their faith. And these data come from the "heart" of the church. Moreover, the computer revealed that within the 53 percent who live with profanity by telling themselves it is "just a habit," there are 37 percent who also chose another option. Thus, even in that group a significant number have mixed feelings. They are not immune to the impact. The fact remains that this is a sore point for many believers. It causes frustration and inner turmoil. When a person is exposed to such an experience on a daily or hourly basis, only a pious fraud can say that it does not undermine the meaningfulness that daily work is supposed to provide in this life.

In fact, profanity at work may serve to remind a number of lay persons of the Name they reverently call upon on Sunday. I do not believe that this is unique to any one body of Christians. When the air is filled with invective, for whatever the reason, it is difficult to escape the difference in spirit from the one in church on Sunday. Obviously the old work ethic has done nothing to make the daily work scene a more God-fearing place.

The frequent use of profanity also causes one to wonder why God becomes the object of such treatment at the workplace. Is it because we have the Eden story in the back of our minds and blame God for the conditions under which we work? Several theological options were part of this question, but very few people selected them. One option suggested that profanity is an expression of Christ's willingness to become a curse for us, to take upon himself our frustration and to join us in weekday work. Another suggested that profanity demonstrates by the hour how we live, move, and have our being in God, since no other historical figures are named in this way. That participants were not drawn to these "explanations" may indicate that an explanation is not good enough. What is more necessary is a change of climate at work, one that will make it not seem so alien or hostile to the Lord of work.

The high incidence of profanity in the workplace and the fact that the data described here are "unprecedented" add a dimension of poignance to the difficulty the church has in facing the sharp contradiction that exists in the experience of the Christian. The poignancy is that the clergy do not have to face it, but the laity must face it day in and day out.

A Deepening Awareness

As shared in the previous chapter, there is another dimension to "shop talk" that confronts believers, one that is on an opposite wavelength from grace and meritorious performance. A decade or so ago writers spoke of the "compartmentalizing" of religion from daily life. The participants in the clue search revealed that some of this persists, but for the majority it is becoming increasingly difficult to keep the two realms separate.

Only one person out of ten keeps grace and the workplace separate in his or her mind. For such persons it is easy to switch gears when they come to church on Sunday. "We are talking about two different worlds." They believe that God's message applies to spiritual not economic matters. For them, going from work to church and back again is like opening and closing a door.

On the other hand, seven out of every ten participants whose daily work is in the world of business and sales indicated that "it is difficult to leave the world's emphasis behind. I am aware of it when sitting in church." What troubles these folks is having to create a need for a product in order to sell it, or being forced by inflation to charge more for a product or service than it is worth. They find help through their faith, but the help faith provides does not resolve the dilemma. The biblical understanding of grace or God's forgiveness is functioning for them when they are in church, but the problem that created the need for grace in the first place is not solved . . . yet.

When business persons return to their stores and counters on Monday, they tend to lose the awareness of God's unmerited favor that was in their minds on Sunday. It fades when they confront the need to work hard and compete during the week. The priorities of daily work seem to rob them of their Sunday words.

The opportunity to share feelings and engage the meaning of these Sunday words in forums and discussion is terribly important, especially if the pulpit is silent about it. There is much to work through here. Thus, when such discussion does occur, one can expect clarification and sharpening of the issues. Such is the nature of communication. For example, in one adult forum where the clue search questions were discussed, one company executive provided further insight into the need he felt to keep his mind free from moral problems when he said, "If someone does not produce, he is not paid. . . . There is no conflict." Another person chimed in, "I see no conflict either. It can't be wrong or anti-Jesus to strive to be my best—either on Sunday or during the week." One cannot quarrel with striving to do or be one's personal best on the athletic field or in the workplace. However, the phrase "one's best" in this adult forum prompted another business person to say, "It's not just a case of doing the best you can, but of doing it better than someone else. Someone has to lose for you to win, much of the time."

Unfortunately, this kind of reality frightened the clergy person who was the leader of this forum, and he soon changed the subject even though people were just getting into it. We should not lose sight of the fact that these lay persons were sharing feelings about their daily lives in church. What better place is there for them to be doing it?

It would seem important that in order to be a whole person one must be the same person at work that one is in church or at home. However, for some lay persons this is a luxury they cannot afford. Forty percent of the people in the trades—carpenters, painters, plumbers, and electricians—said that what they often have to do during the week to survive and what they hear in church on Sunday make them feel like two different persons. One group of people in Minnesota that discussed these questions came to the conclusion that "when threatened in the world outside the church, we would resort to any means to survive."

All of these observations illustrate a deepening awareness of the Sunday/Monday conflict. Perhaps no statement is as clear as that made by the participants who said that the Good News of grace is music to their ears after a week at work. What happens during the week makes them hungry to hear what God has done and is doing for the redemption of humanity. Among the few participants who indicated that they are laborers, this point of view represented 80 percent. For some people the appetite is whetted while they are on the job, but for most of the people who experience hunger for the gospel, the Word begins to speak to them when they arrive in church. A work ethic that would be more consistent with what they hear on Sunday would be helpful for all of these persons. Actually, the climate for change is already present in the underlying feelings to which they gave expression.

It is encouraging to note that this deepening awareness is the effect of the gospel. We will have examples of this in a later chapter, but for now it is in order to observe that when the participants were asked to share some of the dilemmas they face in daily work, one lay person spoke for a number of others when he said that it is only because of the gospel that he feels any dilemma. It is only because of the Word of God that he cares enough to be sensitive. Thus, the gospel is not only a source of comfort but is also the source of their awareness of the incompatibility between Sunday and Monday and the need to bridge the gap.

On Being Partners with Creation

After having applauded the Protestant work ethic for sanctifying work and turning it into "vocation," the writer of the *Time* essay on work went on to say: "In that scheme, the worker collaborates with God to do the work of the universe. . . ."[7] Had the writer really been aware of the ingredients of the work ethic, he would also have mentioned the price we pay for this collaboration. As long as God cooperates and comes through with rewards, the contract is valid and the partnership is intact. However, with inflation and a bloated defense budget eating many out of house and home, the rewards for them have been cut back. We either have to find another basis for faith or stop believing.

Another writer, a clergy person, exalted hard work and then amplified his statement by saying,

> We are not here long, and isn't it kind that while we are here we are given some means of sharing and savoring something of the divine, eternal creativity as we go about our daily [work]? Thank God Michelangelo had an obsessive need to work and that nobody counseled him out of it.[8]

It may be tempting to assume, as this writer did, that such

luminaries as Gandhi, Luther, King, and Mother Teresa were (are) workaholics, and to praise them for it. However, one wonders if it is legitimate to lift up such rare persons as models for humanity. In the field of sports there are some real problems with implying that becoming a superstar like Julius Erving and O.J. Simpson can also happen to a lad who lives in the ghetto of a big city if he just works hard, or that by effort any boy or girl in America can become president.

Moreover, there is an elitist sound to clergy or religious persons being extolled as partners with the Creator or to a clergy person praising that partnership as the nature and purpose of work. It's like listening to someone who has an inside track. In chapter 1 it was said how the Reformation contributed to the concept of a calling. What needs to be pointed out here, however, is that the notion is one to which professional persons relate more easily than do those who are involved in menial tasks or who are out of work. Both a doctor and a sanitation worker contribute to the health and well-being of society, but somehow the doctor's work is thought of as a calling more often than is the work of a garbage man.

Persons in the "helping professions" (doctors, nurses, teachers) are much more inclined to say that they are able to relate grace to their daily work than are those in other walks of life. They also give the reason. They do not see cutthroat competition in the workplace the way persons in business and industry do. And then one doctor added, "Isn't that what the gospel is all about . . . personal relationships?"

The gospel does have to do with personal relationships, but then if somebody's work does not happen to be directly related to helping people or even working with people, he or she has much less chance of experiencing the gospel in daily work. Such persons have a handicap to begin with. A homemaker, for example, contacts other people at the store and perhaps talks with neighbors, but apart from such contacts her or his work is pretty much place oriented, at least until the children get home from school. The work of a painter, carpenter, or machinist is even more place oriented. All three can come into contact with people at lunchtime, but such is not the focus of the brush, the hammer, or the lathe during the rest of the workday.

During the early years of my own pastoral ministry, I used

as an illustration of being partners with God the description of two men who were cutters in a stone quarry. One man hated his work, while the other seemed to find much purpose in it. The difference was that while the first felt as if he was just cutting stone, the second believed that he was helping to build a cathedral. Today, I have second thoughts about this story. I wonder if even the most pious stonecutter thinks only of building a cathedral? If we really knew him and he were honest, would we find that at least on some days he feels more like an inmate pounding rock than a quarryman building a church? Then, too, times change perspectives. There may have been a time when a person working in a stone quarry could feel that he was helping to build a cathedral, but today the feeling may smack more of an "edifice complex" than a partnership with God. Sensing that partnership may have a lot to do with the kind of work in which one is involved.

Perhaps the most dramatic change in the concept of partnership has to do with what it means to be true partners. A real partnership is between equals, and while this could never be true between human beings and God, there is an increasing realization that it is also missing in those who have two good reasons to sense equality: their common humanity and their link with the Creator.

We see and feel an awareness of inequality in the words of an automobile assembly-line worker who described what it was like to get to her job:

> "At the gate you push your way in because there are 20,000 other guys who want to get to work at 7:00 too. Inside you wait for the cattle car (technically known as the 'freight elevator'—the smaller 'passenger elevator' is reserved for white collar workers and bosses)."[9]

Whether we are talking about special elevators, parking places, or unilateral decision making, in such an environment there is no chance of having a partnership with God or "man." There is a missing link in the chain if we are looking for a partnership with the Creator but do not have a partnership with our fellow humans. And for a whopping 86 percent of the participants in the clue search, "having to impress the boss" was very much a force where they work, but the force was negative and demotivating. They might have needed this motivation to get ahead in the company, but something inside of them said that it was demeaning. It took away from the incentive to work. The desire to work *with* others rather than *under* others was making its presence known.

The Holy Spirit in Daily Work

"Just as surely as God desires to lead us to a knowledge of genuine Christian fellowship, so surely must we be overwhelmed by a great disillusionment with others, with Christians in general, and, if we are fortunate, with ourselves." Dietrich Bonhoeffer wrote these words, and then he added, "By sheer grace, God will not permit us to live even for a brief period in a dream world."[10]

Bonhoeffer had in mind people who were looking for a stress-free, extraordinary experience of Christian fellowship, complete with moods of rapture. In the context of this book, so is the church seeking to maintain its separation from the reality of daily work and its tendency, conscious or unconscious, to avoid the sharp contradiction in Christian life.

When we say "church," we have to think of both laity and clergy assembled together for study or worship, for there is ample evidence that lay persons, privately and individually, are painfully aware of the things we have described in this chapter. The God of the Protestant work ethic who rewards some for meritorious service and who chooses some to receive grace but not all, does not exist, and never has, except in human thought. On the other hand, the God of grace and truth has always existed and is very much at work in the thinking of lay persons who on a daily basis confront the realities of the workplace. Thus, if the awareness of the incompatibility between divine grace and a merit-oriented society is deepening, it is a faith experience. Jesus promised that the Spirit would lead us into all truth. There is no justification for assuming that he had in mind only theological insights into doctrinal fine points or programmatic decisions made in ecclesiastical bureaucracies.

Likewise, if church folks feel pain over the high incidence of profanity in the workplace, they are not alone. God, too, feels it there. However, neither the Holy Spirit nor God is inclined toward self-disclosure. God does not trumpet loudly to us, even in church on Easter Sunday. God makes a silent entry into our thoughts. The voice is still and small, usually mingled with our own thoughts, so that we can hardly tell where ours leave off and God's begin.

Nevertheless, there is power through the Spirit when people share aloud together what they are thinking in private concerning what matters to them. We may suffer in silence at work, but we need not do so when we gather together. Indeed, it is a tragedy if we do.

To be open to the Spirit is to be open to the future. For middle- and upper-income folks it means being critical of our economic system rather than protecting the privileges that we garner from it. There is good evidence, which will be presented in the next chapter, that the illusion is over for most of us. The church will only with effort continue to live in a dream world in the area of daily work. The God of grace and truth is active in new ways in the workplace. It is an unprecedented time in which to be alive. However, as Bonhoeffer said, "God is not a God of the emotions but the God of truth. . . . The basis of the community of the Spirit is truth."[11]

Conversation Starters

Daily work is a curse placed upon us because of original sin. Do you agree or disagree? Why?

The meaning we find in our daily work depends on the kind of work we do. Do you agree or disagree? Why?

Profanity is simply a habit and not intended to be disrespectful. Do you agree or disagree? Why?

Why is profanity used so frequently in the workplace?

Why is it harder today to keep church and daily work in separate compartments than it was a decade or two ago?

Is it legitimate to lift up celebrities as models for humanity?

A real partnership is only between equals. Do you agree or disagree? Why?

A partnership with God is difficult to sense if we do not experience a partnership with people with whom we work. Do you agree or disagree? Why?

Being open to the Spirit includes being critical of our economic system. Do you agree or disagree? Why?

Chapter 5

In the Early Hours
of Reformation II

When Frederick Taylor introduced his ideas on scientific management, he referred to the time-and-motion process as a "mental revolution." For many workers, as we have seen in prior chapters, the result was more like psychic numbness. What comes closer to a mental revolution is what is happening now, partly in reaction to the ideas Taylor introduced.

What is happening is like a second Reformation in its early hours, but this time the setting is the workplace, not a church building, and those most involved are the laity, not the clergy. However, the Word is thus still at work.

Like its sixteenth-century counterpart this Reformation first occurred in the thinking of certain individuals even though the climate for change in the workplace is widespread. The fires of the first Reformation did not erupt spontaneously, despite the fact that the "grass" in Germany was very dry.

To highlight the new phenomenon that is occurring in the workplace, a number of examples will be cited in this chapter. The chapter framework, however, will be the dynamics that are at work within these examples.

A New Spirit Is Born

Early in 1983, Howard K. Smith, the retired ABC-TV news-caster, sent out pleas, through radio announcements, for team-work in the marketplace. He cited the decline in productivity and the need to replace competition with cooperation. He offered to provide radio time to any business or corporation that might be attempting to do this. Months went by and all that was heard was his plea, over and over again. Finally in August, on my way to work, I heard him describe a particular company and what it was doing. Then in September another report was given, only this time the owner did the talking. In each case it was obvious that a new spirit was emerging.

Actually, labor-management cooperation first emerged during World War II in response to wartime production demands. In a variety of plants, committees sponsored discussions, suggestion boxes, and other means of eliciting ideas on how to improve production. By the war's end some five thousand committees had formed whose members had agreed to bury the management-union hatchet in the interests of patriotism.

Journalist Stuart Chase thought that an effective committee exposed "a great, rich mine of human effort," but the question was "Will that mine shut down when the war ends?"[1] Not one of the managers and workers he talked to thought so. To a person, they believed that industry had discovered something that was too valuable to lay aside. However, when the cheers on V-E and V-J days faded out, workers and management fell back into their established, adversarial relationships. The glue of patriotism dried up. Still, a new spirit had put in a brief appearance, and the memory was a pleasant one.

Although these labor-management-union committees ceased, a new phenomenon evolved during the post-World War II period and entered the workplace; this was known as "small-group dynamics."

In churches small groups were used to bring new life to youth groups and adult education. The magic number of people in a group was around eight. In a study of church school classes it was found that when the group got much larger, it was better to start a new class. With an increase in numbers came a decrease in verbal participation and interest.[2] Bible study often was done in small groups and even today churches find a new spirit when the right content and method are joined together. Historically, the small group model was one Jesus instituted; on some occasions he spoke to large gatherings, but everyday he talked with the twelve disciples.

The optimum size of groups in the workplace was similar to the size recommended for church groups, but the stated purpose of the groups was strictly task oriented. Their task was to find ways to improve productivity. The more advanced groups did some planning, but the agenda was always set by management. Workers came to feel that their real problems at work were not discussed. The program was called "Organizational Development," but at the General Motors assembly plant in Lordstown, Ohio, "O.D." was referred to derisively as "Overtime and Doughnuts," and not without cause.[3] Despite the name of the program, the hidden agenda of the company was to adjust people to the organization, not vice versa. The structure of the company was a given; workers were to learn skills of group problem solving, listening, and self-discipline in order to function better within it.

The theory was that if the attitudes of workers changed, productivity and organizational structure would improve. However, the unexpected by-product was an awareness that the traditional hierarchical pyramid was antiquated and not meeting the needs of a younger, better educated, and less malleable workforce. Again, however, a new spirit had put in an appearance in the workplace, and as with new wine, the taste once savored was hard to forget.

While idea committees and small groups were springing up in America, a similar phenomenon, but one with added dimensions, was blossoming three thousand miles away in Japan. "Made in Japan" used to be synonymous with shoddy, breakable merchandise. But in a rather short time this phrase has come to symbolize one of the highest standards of quality in the world. Japan currently outproduces the U.S. in cars, Switzerland in watches, Germany in cameras, and Sweden in ships.

Some American business persons became fascinated with the "secrets" of Japanese success. They sent "spies" (who were warmly welcomed) to Japan to find out what was going on. One thing a Ford Motor Company study team discovered was that

80 percent of the Toyotas that came off the assembly line had no defects, whereas they knew the Fords back home averaged seven defects per car. They also found among the workers an enormous capacity for hard work, lifelong employment for many, and an extraordinary level of commitment. The more discerning visitors learned that while there was a certain level of competitiveness between companies, within any one company there was a high level of harmony and cooperation.

The heart and soul of the Japanese spirit, it was learned, stem from teams of workers on the shop floor called quality-control circles. There are over 100,000 of them.[4] These are groups of usually eight to twelve workers, led by a foreman or a senior employee. They meet regularly to address and solve job-related problems. However, in addition to doing the kinds of tasks considered by the committees and small groups in America, they meet to develop internal leadership, to reinforce worker morale and motivation, and to encourage a group spirit that translates into a strong sense of teamwork.

Ironically, the quality-circle idea was brought to Japan after the war by an American, W. Edwards Deming, who defined it in Taylor's terms as the detection of defects. The Japanese took the idea and stood Taylorism on its head. Rather than providing the answers, doing the inspecting, and having an image of omniscience, management moved control and responsibility onto the shop floor. It placed these areas in the hands of those who were closest to the production process—the workers and their supervisors—and made them into teams with common goals.

Today the Japanese bend over backwards to develop a consensus, to communicate horizontally, and to listen to what people have to say; it might appear that this approach is the secret of their team spirit. However, we had two Japanese guests in our home one September evening in 1983, along with an interpreter, and we learned that there may be more to it. It is considered crude in Japan for someone to stand out, to dominate, or to take over. "Thus," said our guests, "if one person has ten talents, he or she will let only five of them be seen. The other five are put to use behind the scenes to help the company and other workers." I asked them if they could think of an illustration of this, and after some thought one of them replied, "If a fast worker finishes a job sooner than expected, he or she will quietly go to the assistance of a slower one so that neither the slow worker nor the department falls behind. But he or she doesn't tell anyone about it or receive more money for doing it."

Initially I thought this process was something unique to Japan, perhaps going back centuries and, like an ID card, nontransferable. However, here in America this has been going on for a long time also. It is indispensable in team sports such as basketball. Someone who hogs the ball or monopolizes the shooting is a detriment to the team. He or she may be a superstar and have great ability but still must work with the team for it to function most effectively. The music world also illustrates this quality. Four soloists singing in a quartette can simply be four soloists. To blend together, each has to be willing to regulate the volume and tune in to the others.

Scripture has its version of this spirit also. We have oneness in Christ, a quality that enables people to rise above differences. In Christ, says Paul, "All things hold together." (See Colossians 1:15-17.)

A New Image Emerges

A new image of the worker as a human being and a resource is emerging in America also. Because management has to change for this to happen, we can speak of a new image of managerial authority emerging at the same time.

Although struggling to the surface in the World War II factory committees and postwar small-group dynamics and implicit in the Japanese quality circles, the new attempt at cooperation between workers and management first showed up here in America in the late 1930s when Joseph Scanlon, an accountant for the LaPointe Steel Company, was asked by its desperate president to help ward off the threat of closure that the company was facing. Scanlon had become known for his belief that no one knew more about the running of a steel mill than those on the shop floor. The task was to find a way of tapping the mental resources of these "experts." What he did was conduct a series of interviews with workers on ways to improve production. The suggestions led directly to the saving of the company.[5]

An admirer of Scanlon, Douglas McGregor, authored an influential postwar book on management. Entitled *The Human Side of Enterprise*, it provided publicity for Scanlon's views and a plan for profit sharing, to which we will return. McGregor put this new image into words. This he did when he described Scanlon's plan as "a formal method providing an opportunity for every member of the organization to contribute . . . brains and ingenuity as well as . . . physical effort to the improvement of organizational effectiveness." He went on to say:

> Even the worker doing repetitive work at the bottom of the hierarchy is potentially more than a pair of hands. He is a human resource. His know-how and ingenuity, properly utilized, may make a far greater difference to the success of the enterprise than any improvement in his physical effort.[6]

Whereas Taylor believed that most people had to be coerced, directed, and threatened with punishment to get them to put forth adequate effort, McGregor believed that people will exercise self-direction and self-control in the service of objectives to which they are committed.

Perhaps most importantly, McGregor believed that the capacity to utilize a relatively high degree of imagination, ingenuity, and creativity in the solution of organizational problems is widely, not narrowly, distributed in the population. Under the conditions of modern industrial life, the intellectual potentialities of the average worker are only partially exercised.[7]

Evidence of workers' capacity to think surfaced in the General Foods pet-food factory in Topeka, Kansas. In an effort to improve the quality of work life in this plant, the company has as its goal that every worker will to be able to do every job in the plant. A visitor to the plant was amazed to find that even workers with little formal education were able to repair sophisticated electronic equipment and computer components in the plant's control room. Moreover, the number of workers there who take advantage of the company's pledge to pay for formal programs of continuing education is three times the average for General Foods as a whole.[8] It would appear that learning on the job has whetted the appetite for more. This presupposes the capacity to think.

The General Motors plant at Lordstown was the scene of one of the most famous walkouts in labor history in February 1972. The issue on the surface was not wages or the right to organize but the quality of work life itself. Actually, the issue was even deeper and more personal. The workers wanted to be treated like human beings. As one of them said, "Some of the machines have written on them, 'Treat Me with Respect and I will give you Top Quality with Less Effort,' and the GM sign. I said we should have that printed on sweatshirts and wear them to work . . . but we wouldn't be able to keep them on for five minutes, we'd be sent home for disrespect."[9] The popularity of Rodney Dangerfield and his "I don't get no respect" quip suggests that this is not only a deep human need, one intimately related to one's self-image, but one of which more and more people today are acutely aware.

The Dana Corporation, which has thirty thousand employees, has become known as a leader in new approaches to corporation management and ownership. Its policies illustrate beautifully the emergence of a new image in the workplace. These policies are described on a single page, which replaced a stack of "corporate procedures." The first four paragraphs emphasize the importance of profits for shareholders and of a steady growth rate. The eleven remaining paragraphs are about people. These paragraphs declare that at Dana "we are dedicated to the belief that our people are our most important asset."[10]

Frances Heaps, president of International Group Plans, a direct-mail group health insurance company, goes even further. He observes that he "does not consider health insurance by direct mail [to be] IGP's main product. 'I consider our main product the participation of people in decision-making in their workplace. It is their right to grow as human beings.' The real objective of the business is making life a little better for the people who are involved—the employees, the suppliers, and the clients—not corporate profits and employee income."[11]

What we have in this new image is a workplace application of the Reformation's "priesthood of believers" doctrine and Martin Luther's belief that the work of the scrubwoman or the milkmaid is—in God's sight—equal to that of the monk, and hence should be so in the sight of "man" as well. When the worker is seen as a resource for solving problems, and so on, he or she is as important to the company as the president and all the levels of management in-between.

Levels of Ownership

Having a voice in decisions that affect our daily work reflects a significant level of ownership, one that forecaster John Naisbitt describes as a "megatrend." He sees large numbers of citizens, workers, and consumers demanding and receiving a greater voice in government, business, and the marketplace. The U.S. workplace as a totalitarian fiefdom, where workers must check their rights at the gate, is declining. Pressure from courts and legislatures is causing companies to welcome worker participation in decision making because it is now in their economic interest to do so. While the motive is not the best, response to this pressure is a reality.

Justification for calling this a "megatrend" comes from the process employed in perceiving it. Daily newspapers in cities with a population greater than 100,000 are read carefully by Naisbitt and his colleagues and their contents analyzed. Collectively, these newspapers reach 94 percent of the total U.S. population every day. All local hard-news items are then clipped and sorted into categories. Clippings from particular categories are read by the same persons each month, so changes tend to jump out at them. Also, the number of lines devoted to each topic are counted, and changes over a period of time are noted. This counting provides a quantitative way of measuring change in societal concerns and priorities. When analysts sit down and compare notes, changes in one category are related to changes in another and the megatrend is perceived.[12]

Direct feedback from the workplace on this level of ownership comes from Harvey Davis, executive director of the International Association of Quality Circles, who said that the idea of vocal participation answers deeper psychological needs of workers than are usually recognized. What is known is that more than 750 U.S. companies have installed an average of ten quality circles apiece, prompting Davis to observe, "This concept will operate in any industry, manufacturing or service, and in any culture."[13]

Another level of ownership related to giving workers a voice is reached when managers share information with them. Most managers tend not to give out information, assuming that workers do not need to know. However, Marvin Woskow, executive vice-president of Denka, a large chemical company in Houston, indicates that there is an insatiable desire for information in quality circles. "I don't care if you work for General Motors, or Ford, or here, you want to know how things are going, first off with the unit, and secondly with the company as a whole."[14] Dana, the company that views people as its most important asset, requires its managers to keep its employees up-to-date through newsletters, bulletin boards, group meetings, and one-on-one communication.

Giving people a voice and information builds trust. Nothing is more destructive of trust than executives who feel that unilateral decisions and the information that leads to them are their business, their prerogative, alone, and that by exercising this prerogative, they protect people from being bothered by details.

Ownership leads to motivation. Rene McPherson, Dean of Stanford Business School, observes, "We don't motivate people. They are motivated by their upbringing, education and other things. . . . What we are doing is taking the handcuffs off by giving the workers responsibility and a voice in how their jobs are done."[15]

It stands to reason that when people have a vested interest in their work, motivation will increase. Thus, it is not surprising to hear the chief executive of a large bank in Stockholm, a bank with five thousand people employed in five hundred branches and twenty district offices, observe that there is no trade-off between the objectives of democracy and efficiency. More democracy leads to better performance. Democracy raises the level of trust and releases ideas and energy that transforms the organization.[16] Democracy may take longer, but once a decision is reached democratically, the initiative and incentive that emerge more than make up for "lost time."

Sharing ownership, however, can involve more than giving people a voice, information, and responsibility. It also can reach the level of having employees own a share in the company's stock or share in the profit. Joseph Scanlon, whose plan saved a company, devised a way to tie profit sharing to improved productivity. Seventy-five percent of any surplus is returned to the employee group and divided in proportion to each one's salary or wage. Since the plan rewards the group rather than the individual, the pressure to produce comes from peers rather than from the insistence of management. By 1980 there were at least five hundred active "Scanlon plans" across the country modeled after the system he had invented for LaPointe, but mostly at plants with fewer than one thousand employees. One possible reason for the failure of the plan to gain even wider acceptance may be managerial fears of losing control.[17]

To some, profit sharing sounds like communism. However, in February 1975, a radio speaker noted that over the next ten years there would probably be five hundred billion dollars' worth of new investment for businesses and industrial expansion. He asserted that "it can also be five hundred billion dollars' worth of corporate ownership by employees." He then drew this conclusion: "Could there be a better answer to Karl Marx than millions of workers individually sharing in the ownership of the means of production?"[18] That speaker was Ronald Reagan.

An American superintendent at the Japanese-owned Quasar television manufacturing plant in Franklin Park, Illinois, said, "The Japanese feel that the worker is the money-maker."[19] There are many managers and owners of corporations in America who feel that those who have put their hard-earned money into a business enterprise have a right to enjoy the fruits of that enterprise and to say how they are divided. This is a sacred premise for those who defend *inequality* in the workplace. While it may indeed be true that the owner had to work hard to accumulate the initial investment for rebuilding or expanding a plant, the success of the new investment will be possible only because of the hard work of the people he or she has hired. "Once new investment has been made, there is no longer the same basis for saying that the original owner has the right to control the entire product of the new investment." According to the logic of hard work, "The workers should have a right to appropriate an ever increasing share of the product."[20]

A Redistribution of Power

"... The rulers of the Gentiles lord it over them. ... It shall not be so among you; but whoever would be great among you must be your servant ... even as the Son of man came not to be served but to serve. .." (Matthew 20:25-28).

Jesus was talking here about a redistribution of power. When it comes to introducing democracy into the workplace, the transition from boss to colleague is imperative. What happens when the leader serves as a resource rather than an order-giver is that we visually reverse the organizational chart. "Our hierarchy is just like that of any other plant," said Dennis Butt at Kawasaki. "Our organizational structure is the same except that I just turned it upside down. My position is on the bottom of the chart and the hourly worker's is on top. We consider the hourly worker the top of the organization and everyone else is here to support him or her."[21]

Executives who are interested in introducing democracy into their workplace may think that they can simply hire someone to come in and do this for them without their own personal involvement in change, but such is not the case. David Easlick, president of Michigan Bell Telephone, was one who realized that any change in company policy or structure would first have to begin with himself. He described his change as "from supreme warlord, order giver, and chief idea man to someone closer to being a colleague, listener and cooperator."[22] He had three qualities necessary for a participatory leader: first, the curiosity in how he might improve his organization; second, the capacity to acknowledge that he was a major part of the problem; and third, his willingness to change his managerial style and practice.[23]

The most paradoxical figure in the move toward workplace democracy is the leader. In every situation, top-management support is vital for the initiation and ultimate success of reformation. Where such reform has occurred, the leader has viewed the redistribution of power, not as a surrender, but as a sharing—a gain not a loss. Moreover, sharing power and decision making is not a sign of weakness but of strength, says Pehr Gyllenhammar, president of Volvo. "The weak are incapable of delegating and have every reason to fear sharing their power. The strong have the self-confidence that makes delegation possible and easy."[24]

Change of any magnitude frightens people. Those with power are reluctant to share it. They will find lots of reasons why they should not do so. They will even say that workers don't really want more responsibility. Where genuine participation has emerged, a change in power relationships has been inevitable. Business under a more democratic system is not "as usual."

The difficulty [here] cannot be overestimated. The solitary ascent through the ranks of an existing hierarchy is [by conventional thought] success. Why should people who have struggled to the

top think of changing? . . ."The typical manager is over-educated, over-energized, pretty confident and dynamic. *That* is the person to whom you are going to say, 'Let the people decide'?". . .
Most managers, if asked, would say they are already participatory. They consult their subordinates about many decisions.[25]

"Consultation," however, is a long way from what is happening in those companies to which we have referred in this chapter, companies where true democracy is emerging.

One executive's style of leadership is to let his department heads and personal assistants share their views at cabinet meetings, and then he decides; or after they have all shared their views, he shares his view and it is decisive. He would say, as do his assistants, that he is truly listening. However, not even such listening changes the spirit in the organization, or the self-image of staff persons under him. It does not effect a redistribution of power.

Even those executives who are strongly in favor of sharing their power and authority can experience distress and the need for patience and support at the level of middle management. If their job is telling people what to do, they are not likely to favor asking people what they think.

Increased worker participation can frequently lead to the elimination of whole layers of middle managers. . . . The participatory leader delights in increased efficiency but is sympathetic to the people being displaced. Rene McPherson said, "You don't fire them. You put them somewhere where they can [handle the responsibility]. . . . You keep your arm around them in public and don't lower their compensation. *They* didn't change the system. You did."[26]

Then, too, corporate specialists and technicians—personnel managers, lab chemists, quality-control persons, and engineers—at corporate levels can find not having their professional kinsmen to talk to frustrating. When workers do jobs formerly held by middle management persons, people calling in and wanting to speak with them can become disconcerted. However, when this happens, it can also be a revelation of Reformation II. An example is a General Foods manager at one plant calling up the Topeka plant, asking for the personnel manager or lab technician, and hearing a voice say, "I'm it for this week."

When you come right down to it, there are not many places in society where people can work together democratically or gain experience along these lines. Most people have never had any such experience. They seldom get it at school, and never in the army or at work. They might not even experience it in their families. Thus, the church becomes one arena where people can gain this experience, providing, of course, that the leaders in the church, both clergy and lay leaders, are themselves committed to the sharing of power and decision making. However, it is quite clear that Reformation II has not depended upon church officialdom to give it support or approval.

The Importance of Motives

Last, but far from least, among the dynamics that are shaping what we are calling a workplace reformation are the motives for management's interest in or implementation of worker participation. Actually, the reader had an early exposure to this topic when we were describing the use of small groups at the GM plant in Lordstown, Ohio. It was a problem of motive that caused workers there to speak derisively of "Organizational Development" as "Overtime and Doughnuts." The motives of the company were showing when the small groups were used to adjust the worker to the company or to improve production rather than to help the workers with what they considered to be the real problems on the job.

While beneath the surface and sometimes unconscious, motives often show through words and actions. The agenda, though hidden, can be quite transparent to the worker. Workers naturally become suspicious of the reasons for introducing democracy in the workplace after the jobs of some colleagues have been automated out from under them.

One of the examples of how motives can begin to speak occurred when General Foods tried to make its plant at Topeka into a model of worker democracy. Time clocks were removed. Employees were organized into teams of eight to sixteen persons with significant control over hiring and promotion of fellow workers. Jobs were rotated, and team members where chosen to be coaches not foremen, to lead by example not by direction.

When they listened to journalists, "change agents," and sympathetic managers, the workers at first believed what they were hearing. But when the enthusiasm wore off, many workers

looked around and asked what the benefits really were. "We
were in the clouds for a long time," said one worker. "But 300
tons of dog food a day, every day, can bring you down to earth
in a hurry."[27]

Workers realized that the basic decision, the one concerning
quantity, was only a mimic of what management had already
decided, or would have decided. As one employee observed
bitterly, "You get right down to the fact that they [management]
can do whatever they want. They run it. They own it. . . . What
rights do I have? I mean, they didn't even have to let us do this
whole thing in the first place. That plant is there for one reason—
to make money."[28]

Some managerial people are up front about motives. Imperial
Chemical Industries, a large company in Great Britain, sought
to implement some worker-democracy ideas, but they admitted
that they were not interested in changing the world or in creating
a new era in worker-management relations. They sought to
involve workers in decisions, not because they wanted them to
"self-actualize," but because the more alert and committed the
workers were, the better would be their performance. Although
this may not be saying that the motive for the change is to make
money, at least it is being honest about the reasons for incor-
porating the change.

According to the writers of *Working Together*, "Managers and
workers are changing their ways of working not because it is
'good' but because it is good business. Necessity thus becomes
the mother of cooperation as well as invention."[29] However, the
writers also admit that it is difficult to develop a common purpose if "the bottom line" and "company loyalty" are the major
motivating factors. "The company is only worth supporting if
it serves society," a Volvo manager said. "When we overvalue
organization as an end, not a means, it becomes an idol."[30]

Profit is still the number one motive for most business and
industrial enterprises, and perhaps many managers would say
that controls on profits will destroy incentive to work. However,
what emerges in this chapter is that the managers are speaking
for themselves. There are many in the workplace who find other
incentives more motivating. Indeed, in his study of leadership,
Michael Maccoby found that "for most managers, organizational
development is evaluated solely in terms of productivity and

profit. Paradoxically, this total concern for profit is what causes distrust and limits efficiency. People only trust leaders who articulate a moral code, who care about people. . . ."[31]

Even if a manager does not set out to democratize decision making but only to try and manage more effectively, when he or she looks back at what has taken place, he or she will often find that greater participation and equality among people has resulted. And few managers would revert to a former way of working with people. It may be that they gain new insight in viewing the results, which in turn illuminates and purifies the original reason for making the change.

The direction in which the workplace reformation is leading is summed up well in the words of James Lincoln, founder of Lincoln Electric, which for a long time was the only company in America with a public guarantee of lifelong employment. Lincoln quoted the Worker whose motives were pure, "As ye would that others would do to you do ye even so to them." (See Luke 6:31.) He then went on to say that this "is the complete answer to all problems that can arise between people. The Christian philosophy of life is complete. Our reaction to it is the problem. We do not easily change our developed habits. The acceptance of such change is the problem, not the development of a proper program."[32]

Because the saying of Jesus is called the "golden rule," there is a tendency in theological circles to denigrate it as "law" rather than to see it as "gospel." However, it quickly becomes part of the Good News when we think of doing to others what we would like them to do to us as one motive for God providing salvation through Jesus. The "golden rule" then becomes an expression of God's graciousness in a horizontal form. Whether law or gospel, this teaching is making its presence felt in the workplace, and it makes the Protestant work ethic pale in comparison.

Conversation Starters

What accounts for the different images of workers in the minds of Taylor and McGregor?

Why have persons in managerial positions tended to view workers as persons who prefer not to think?

Is it really possible for a company to put its people ahead of its profit?

How is shared ownership in the means of production an answer to Karl Marx?

What signs of change in managerial style are showing up where you work or have worked?

Turning the organizational chart upside down can be done only on paper. Do you agree or disagree? Why?

The total concern for profit causes distrust and limits efficiency. Do you agree or disagree? Why?

Why are hidden agendas to increase productivity so apparent to employees?

Do you think that the "golden rule" is law or gospel?

Chapter 6

Grace:
God's Work Ethic

The Protestant work ethic began with the need for people to prove the validity of God's grace by working hard and achieving a substantial income. This left God with little to do but let people think that human effort or faith would be rewarded. Reformation II draws upon the true meaning of grace and reveals—with the help of Scripture—God acting within us and among us.

In his book *Psychological Economics*, George Katona wrote how difficult it is for most people consciously to sustain feelings of anger, hostility, or frustration for any length of time.[1] Something at work within us enables most of us to cool off. Things that look pretty grim at night don't seem so bad in the morning. It's as if the One who neither slumbers nor sleeps heals our minds while our bodies rest.

Biblical Precedent

Jeremiah pointed thought in this direction when he wrote that the mercies of God are "new every morning."[2] Some would say God's mercy only *looks* new. It was present the night before also, but we were less prepared to appreciate it. During the night the grace of God does not change. We do. Both grace and a sunrise signify a fresh start. We may return to the same problems, even the same sins, but there is something about a new day that makes the grace of God more real and we have no reason to assume that it must come to an abrupt halt after breakfast.

Other biblical illustrations of grace relating to daily work show up in both the Old and New Testaments. One that often goes unnoticed or is left unarticulated appears in the parable of Jesus concerning the father who had two sons. (See Luke 15:11-32.) While the words Jesus used did not include the phrase "work ethic," the old attitude appeared in the words Jesus placed in the mouths of both sons.

We see it first in the words of the younger son who found himself living in poverty and disgrace after squandering his share of the inheritance. Waking up one morning in a foreign city, he realized that his father's servants were better off than he was. He decided to return home in hopes that his father would hire him and let him work his way back into the good graces of his parent.

The other son revealed elements of the old work ethic when in response to his father's welcome-home party for his younger brother he said, "All these years I have been faithful to you. I have done everything you asked me to do, but you never gave me a party!" The older son's words, regardless of the Bible translation, reflect his belief that hard work was the way to his father's heart and that one day he would be rewarded. He felt his father owed him something for his steady effort, his stewardship, and he resented his brother having received something for nothing. We do not know how much he had thought prior to his brother's return about a reward for service rendered, but the implication is that it had been on his mind. It certainly was on the mind of Jesus, the storyteller.

The tendency of biblical scholars and preachers to spiritualize this story, to say it only illustrates the grace of God, robs it of the work ethic context that gives God's grace both meaning and relevance. The father's welcome to the wayward son was in stark contrast to the attitudes of both sons toward daily work. Both saw work as something they had to do to earn a share of their father's good will. On the other hand, the response of the father to both sons revealed the way in which God's grace or

Grace: God's Work Ethic 87

favor assumes other forms such as compassion, acceptance, approval, reinforcement, and encouragement.

The Bible has other illustrations of the grace in God's work ethic. In Leviticus 25 there is a description of what was to happen every fifty years in the Hebrew nation. The fiftieth year was to be a year for all who had lost property due to hard times. Those unable to maintain payments were to have their debt canceled and their land restored to them. It was to be a year of liberty, understandably called one of "jubilee," at least for the poor. Directions on the prices of crops in proportion to one's ability to pay were also a part of the plan. From this Scripture passage one gets a feeling for Jesus' use of the term "liberty." Early in his ministry he spoke of liberty for the poor and oppressed. (See Luke 4:16-21.) Although Jesus was in the synagogue when he quoted this statement from Isaiah, it is directly related to the daily work scene from which income is derived.

Although Christians have a tendency to think of the Old Testament as law oriented rather than grace oriented, there are places in the Old Testament, such as those we have mentioned, where grace shines through the regulations. Another shows up in Exodus 33:19, where the Lord declared, "I will be gracious to whom I will be gracious." An intriguing exposition of this verse appears in the rabbinic literature written between the times of the Testaments.

In that hour God showed Moses all the treasuries of the rewards which are prepared for the righteous. Moses said, "For whom is *this* treasury?" and God said, "For him who fulfills the commandments." "And for whom is *that* treasury?" "For him who brings up orphans." And so God told him about each treasury. Finally, Moses spied a big treasury and said, "For whom is that?" And God said, "To him who has nothing I give from *this* treasury"; as it is said, "I will be gracious to whom I will be gracious and I will show mercy on whom I will show mercy."[3]

In the New Testament there is a parable of Jesus that seems to take its cue from the above Exodus passage. It is the parable our lunchroom friends at Bethlehem Steel (in chapter 3) were discussing—about the vineyard owner who went out at different times of the day and hired people who were not working. Near the end of the day he went out again and came across some men standing idle. When he inquired why they were not working, they replied, "Because no one has hired us." (See Matthew 20:7.) It is obvious from their response and from that of the vineyard owner, seen through the eyes of Jesus, that God was moved by unemployment in the first century. Clearly, Jesus chose to use this very real situation to illustrate God's work ethic. People who had been overlooked or who were stigmatized as lazy were paid the same wage as those who had no trouble getting a job. One can't help but feel that Jesus understands the unemployed black men standing on a Harlem street corner, even though he did not articulate these feelings specifically.

Once again, however, many scholars and preachers are inclined to spiritualize the story, to say it has but one point, which is that the generosity of the vineyard owner is analogous to the generosity of God. We do this to avoid a biblical interpretation in which someone attaches significance to a minute aspect of the parable, thereby distorting it and perhaps even losing sight of the central point the parable is trying to convey.

In the case of this parable it is difficult to avoid our feeling that the pay scale in the parable is embarrassing, if not impossible to relate to the American workplace. Thus, it becomes a necessity to ignore or remove the first-century situation that gave rise to it. However, it may be that even those with such hesitation will admit that part of the work attitude is extremely relevant, namely, the part wherein those who worked all day are upset when everybody is paid the same. The all-day workers, who had indeed agreed to their wage, illustrate the old work ethic, that those who work longer and harder deserve more, regardless of any circumstances affecting the unemployed.

Having let this much of the first-century situation into our time, we find it difficult not to acknowledge what really bugs us: by paying all workers the same wage, the vineyard owner made the "others equal to them," as Jesus put it. Jesus and a contemporary scholar are aware of the way in which the self-worth and identity of the disgruntled workers can depend upon their comparing themselves with those worse off. The disgruntled workers see themselves as superior to the unemployed. The vineyard owner challenged this self-image when he focused attention on the plight of the unemployed and on why they were unemployed. Both were implicit in his concern. Neither of these issues was of concern to those who had worked all day.[4]

God's work ethic, on the other hand, is based on grace, and grace takes into account the historical situation in which people find themselves. Especially in the light of God's concern for being gracious to whom he chooses to be gracious, it is an untimely distortion of this parable to extract from it a message about God's generosity and ignore the context in which that message was communicated. Moreover, it is hard to believe that one who came to declare Good News to the poor and liberty to the oppressed just happened to select a work-employment setting for a parable. It is hard to believe that he just dreamed up this setting. But it is easy to believe that he had observed these conditions in the first century and wished to comment on the relation of God's grace to people affected by them. The fact remains that Jesus Christ chose real life situations as the vehicles for his teaching. Therefore, we dare not turn the situation in this parable into an abstraction.

Forms of Grace at Work Today

Against the backdrop of this biblical witness to the graciousness of God's work ethic, and also sensing the newness of each day, we now consider some of the forms grace is assuming now in weekday work.

A Sunday/Monday Breakthrough

We observed in earlier chapters that, in order to compete effectively in the world of weekday work, many members of the laity have had to leave their understanding of grace as undeserved favor at the door of the church when they leave it on Sunday or at the door of their homes when they leave them on Monday. We have considered the effects of this on lay faith and life. What has happened in Reformation II amounts to a breakthrough in closing the gap between what occurs in church on Sunday and what occurs in daily work on Monday.

This breakthrough is surfacing in the new image of both worker and management. It represents a 180-degree turn, an about face. This new image emerges not only in corporation executives who turn the manager-worker grid upside down, but also in management people who listen to workers.

When Dennis Butt of Kawasaki says that he perceives his role to be one of supporting the hourly wage earners and putting them at the top, we come very close to the concept of a servant, to which both Jesus and the Bible point. When this is related to God, an incarnational ring is heard. When someone asks, "Who does he think he is, God Almighty?" it is not a compliment. This question reveals an image of God that is above and aloof. Jesus Christ reversed this by assuming human form in God's name and living and working with us. This kind of dynamic is released in a corporation when the people on top and in executive positions listen to workers, truly support their efforts, and share the decision-making power and the profits. Even those who use the new relationship for strictly economic gain could do so only after the new image had emerged, not before.

A Deep-Voiced Prophet

The breakthrough did not occur by itself. The soil was there, but human farmers helped to plant seeds and did some rather powerful cultivating. There are a number of individuals who are currently doing just this in the United States, but none is more colorful than W. Edward Deming, the man mentioned in the previous chapter as having brought the idea of quality circles to Japan. He is a daily-work version of John the Baptist; on an even "higher" plane, some who meet him come away with the enthusiasm of those who have met the Savior.[5]

John was not known for eloquence and wisdom when he went about preaching, and these areas are not Deming's forte either. Truth would seem to be more his point. He is the same age as this century—85—and when he goes around the country giving top management persons a four-day workshop on managerial policies and practices, he has been known to tell the same story six times. When he came to Philadelphia early in 1984, a church-member friend of ours was among the 360 participants. Although he admitted being sold on Deming's ideas at the end of day one, neither he nor any of the 359 others were missing when the curtain came down on day four.

Speaking in deep bass tones, Deming starts right out blasting American corporation policies as stupid. He delivers sledgehammer, John-the-Baptist-type blows at the thickheadedness of

American management, and in five minutes the hundreds of participants know he is talking about them. They may feel anger toward him at first, but they know he is right. He is speaking the truth, and his message comes at a point when there is a deep sense of need in the American business world. Deming's ideas are those whose time has come.

His tone may seem like the opposite of grace, and his message may not seem to convey unmerited favor. Yet, there is grace in his judgment. Participants know there in no other way, and after four days many go away believing that to follow what Deming says will mean the salvation of their company and their future. He has indeed done them an undeserved favor.

Deming is a powerful advocate of the untapped potential among and within workers. He challenges the managerial image that workers are lazy, unmotivated, and unintelligent. "Even a fifth grader can understand this," he thunders at the highest echelon of America's corporations, and somehow his listeners get the feeling that again he has deliberately reversed the conventional imagery of labor and management.

Eliminating Fear

A major theme in Deming's "gospel" is that corporate policies are designed to scare workers and are counterproductive. These policies include rules, regulations, inspections, and annual performance reviews. It is interesting to observe that casting out fear is high on the Lord's agenda also.

Deming preaches that the effects of merit rating systems or management by objectives are devastating. Such practices destroy teamwork and nurture rivalry. They build fear and leave colleagues bitter and despondent, sometimes unfit for work for weeks after the experience. In the clue search it was found that 70 percent of those surveyed believe that instilling fear of the penalty for failure is company policy. Thus we can see some fertile soil for Deming's message. For many people these are the early stages of Reformation II. But everything has a beginning, and this one is grace at work.

Things happen when people get the message. When Rene McPherson became president of Dana, he met with the board of directors.

McPherson took the 13-inch-thick stack of corporate procedures and set them down on the board table. Those policies, he said, were written for only 10 percent of the Dana employees and got in the way of the other 90 percent. Which ones should be retained? The chairman said there were several "important" ones to be kept and McPherson asked him to specify. "Oh, I never had the time to read them," was the answer. After a few minutes of discussion, McPherson dropped the entire stack into a wastebasket and promised to bring to the next meeting all that was needed on one sheet. He did, and the Dana board never looked back.[6]

As was noted in the previous chapter, that single sheet is devoted to describing the value the company now places on its people.

Doing away with fear means allowing room for failure, and this concept, too, is putting in a timely appearance in Reformation II. In describing how the Jones and Laughlin Steel Corporation increased production at a Cleveland mill by 20 percent, the president said success came from "deep delegation" of authority to superintendents, which left them "free to make big mistakes."[7] Since decision making is also at the mill floor level, workers, too, are in the position of asserting initiative, stumbling, recovering, and trying again.

"Failure" in the workplace, however, may pertain to failure to measure up to company standards or to what the company considers "sin," for instance, losing a sale or not meeting a deadline. If so, it is more of a sin against the stockholders or the profit motive than against God. Moreover, we do not know if these daily-work failures are the sins that are confessed in church on Sunday. Nonetheless, however secular such sins may seem, wherever they are forgiven—in church or weekday work— grace is there also. Daily life, not one hour in church on Sunday, is the arena wherein the Word of God's unmerited mercy applies; wherever support for failure shows up, it is unmerited, undeserved. Such is the nature of failure. Such is the nature of grace.

Under the Influence

In Dr. Deming's view one of management's cardinal sins is exhortation. Executives who paste slogans on the walls such as "Zero Defects!" or "Be a Quality Worker" or "Do It Right the First Time," are at best misguided. At worst they imply that workers need to be prodded or admonished. In this context might fall what he considers "man's lowest degradation"—piecework.[8]

The echo of McPherson's words rings in our ears. "We don't motivate people. They are motivated by their upbringing, education and other things. . . . What we are doing is taking the handcuffs off. . . ."[9] In the clue search the most frequent response to a question on work incentives was satisfaction from "doing a job well." Nobody has to tell people to do that.

What this says is that motives other than greed are alive in the human spirit. Capitalists who think that controls on profit making would destroy the incentive to work just do not know people, or themselves, very well. Grace is not given just to a few, to an elite group of believers who meet in church. Everybody who gets up in the morning is under the influence, and as we said, grace does not come to an end after breakfast. There is no need to think that if the exhortation is removed, workers will cease being motivated.

One of the saddest commentaries on the faith of the church is that for many who profess faith in the redemption we have in Christ, sin is still at the center of life. Fear of human nature replaces faith in the Good News of grace and the motivation that issues from it.

Paul encountered the same thing in the first century when some said that grace would encourage people to sin; it would lead to moral laxity in the world. (See Romans 6:1-4.) Paul's experience was that grace contained both motivation and constraint. There is a sense in which grace is both demand and deliverance. It can make us aware of our sin and pardon it at the same time. Where it has a chance to work, it does not remove from us a sense of responsibility; it creates one.

Quality Support

It follows that if workers are under the influence of grace when they assemble in small groups to solve problems and find mutual support, then problem solving and mutual support can be expected to happen. The quality circles that are emerging are the "sacraments" of the workplace, and they have "Reformation" sanction. In the sixteenth century the reformers referred to lay channels as the "mutual consolation and conversation of the brethren."[10] Such was considered a means of grace. Although this may have had a church-building orientation then, today it is occurring at the workplace.

Sharing the Good News of God's free grace may be a privilege of the pulpit, but it is God's grace that is proclaimed, not the pulpit's or the preacher's. Paul may plant and Apollo water, but God gives the increase; this makes the workplace an extension of the church building, the location of the church during the week.

If church members do not have this kind of a support-group atmosphere at work, such a group would be a natural thing for a congregation to provide or to become. It would be a way of truly "equipping the saints" or of ministering to the workplace. And if there are enough members or friends from a congregation or from a cluster of congregations that are in a similar field of work, the group could have an additional common bond. More will be said about this in the last chapter.

Justice Through Grace

Grace has also emerged in the guise of justice. We say "guise" because there are those in the workplace who say that justice is a two-way street. High achievers have as much right to exercise their talent and power as those without power have a right to be treated as human beings. Thus, justice is not enough. When there is only justice, the situation is like that of the elephant dancing among the chickens and saying, "Everyone for himself." Where the conditions are not equal to begin with, something more is needed. Grace is needed, and grace emerges from both directions.

Grace has been at work for a long time in the capacity of the powerless to endure their situation. It is also present where those with few talents have to compete with those of many talents in the name of free enterprise. When David Hoekema writes that "the prosperity the rest of us enjoy depends on their willingness to suffer hardship," he is really talking about grace flowing from the bottom of the economic system to those at the top.[11] However, grace has also emerged in Reformation II in the form of certain "elephants" sharing their power, realizing perhaps that their power is given to lift others not to hold them down.

Job Security

Another form of grace at work is job security, for which there is an excellent example in the Hewlett-Packard electronics firm in Palo Alto, California. In an interview William Hewlett stated that both he and Dave Packard were products of the depression. They saw what happened then and did not want a hire-and-fire workplace. The two men also knew what it was like to do routine, menial tasks. Having done everything from sweeping floors to keeping the books, they knew people and could sympathize with their problems. When an employee came down with tuberculosis at a time when the company did not have health insurance, the employers assisted him. Subsequently, they took out coverage for everyone. When orders fell in 1970 and they faced laying off 15 percent of their people, they decided instead to cut one full day for everyone every two weeks. All employees, including executives, voluntarily took a 15 percent pay reduction. Everyone shared the burden, and in six months they were back to normal.[12] Burden bearing was very much a part of what Jesus came to implement, and when it takes place, whether in the congregation assembled in the church building or in the congregation assembled at the workplace, grace is making God's presence felt.

Grace and Automation

All the checkout clerk at the supermarket has to do now is to pass a package over a scanner, and the name of the item and the price are automatically recorded on the cash register tape. This is but a tiny step in the advancement in technology that is hitting the shores of America like a tidal wave from the sea. Some call it the Second Industrial Revolution, giving rise to the iron-collar class—robots. One computer instructor compared where we are now in the technology of automation to where the Wright brothers were in the building of airplanes.

Speaking more modestly, others refer to a movement in our economy from the production of goods to information. It sounds like de-industrialization, a revolution in reverse. There are predictions that in two decades the people employed in information will be 85 percent of the workforce.[13] Included in this figure, however, are all the service workers who have been in the yellow pages for years. Now, it is said, craftsmen, plumbers, and auto mechanics are, in effect, selling information.

What the effect really is for some is to take the work out of work, the drudge out of drudgery. While the great majority of industrial tasks are currently beyond the capacity of robot technology, progress is being made. It is believed, for example, that in the 1990s robots may be able to respond to sensory cues, acquire skills, and transfer these skills to other robots.

Major changes may occur in factories and in construction work as the iron-collar workers carry materials, position walls and floors, lay bricks, take inventory, and manage tools, machining, finishing, inspection, and production. Human work in factories and at construction sites will be a spectator sport.

White-collar workers will be affected as well as blue-collar workers. There is no indication that the computer transformation of existing jobs will create demands for increasingly sophisticated work skills. Quite the contrary is projected. New technologies will further simplify and routinize work tasks and reduce the need for worker individuality and judgment. When computers are able to respond to requests for information from the sound of a voice and to reply in kind, even the need for expertise in gaining access to the information will be reduced.

However, on a more realistic note, everyone will not benefit from this new age, despite utopian forecasts. There will still be a need for service workers to expend human effort. Members of the pink-collar force will still have to learn how to use word-processing machines. The supermarket checkout clerk still has to lift the cans and packages from one end of the counter to the other. Fast-food workers may merely touch a control panel to record an order, but someone still has to prepare it, wrap it, and hand it to the customer, who still has to eat it.

Robert Kondracki, principal of the Southeastern Vocational Technical School in Easton, Massachusetts, noted how all of the trades will be affected by computer technology. His machine shop will be the first to feel it, but soon the school will have a robot department. However, he did not believe that robots would replace carpenters, painters, and electricians, but will assist them in serving the needs of the public.

Some manual labor, such as rubbish collecting, would seem not to be affected at all. It is hard to visualize robots moving up

and down the streets emptying containers and picking up bags
of leaves. Actually, when it comes to the employment picture,
there are mixed forecasts. It is predicted that by the end of the
decade up to 75 percent of all factory jobs will be gone. The
epidemic of unemployment will get worse and could jump to
20 percent by 1990, say some.[14] It will soon be impossible to
pretend that economic recovery is solving the problem; the whole
technological base is undergoing a transformation.

On the other hand, there are others who predict a host of
new jobs. It will take an army of people to convert large industries to a robot-based operation. It may even take the army itself.
Anticipating tension between the affluent information-rich and
the unskilled information-poor, Barry Jones, Australia's Minister
for Science and Technology, proposes a National Labor Force
Planning Commission that will seek to generate new types of
employment complementary to but not dependent upon technology. These should be labor/time absorbing. He sees future
work expansion in such areas as education, tourism, subsistence
farming, material recycling, and nature-related work.[15]

It is in relation to these various components of the computer
age that the need for a work ethic based on grace is seen. The
old work ethic that rewarded hard work or knowledge will be
passé for many people. Watching a computer or a robot will not
make people work up a sweat—unless the air conditioning goes
off—and when the knowledge of the world is stored on a chip
the size of a finger nail, education will have more to do with
learning how to gain access to this information than it will have
to do with reading books or knowing how to think. What is
received as monetary reward (salary) will have been unearned
or unmerited. Income for many will seem more like a gift.

Society's thinking about wages and work will undergo a
change. It may become increasingly difficult to pay someone
less who is working at a noncomputerized job, when she or he
will be the only one left actually doing "hard work" anymore.

As long as machines produce an equivalent of human-pro-
duced wealth, we will be none the poorer. We may even be
better off—materially. We must create a system of distribution
that will ensure that the needs of all for goods and services are
fairly met. It would be monstrously unfair and lacking in grace
or justice if a technological "luck of the draw" were to favor a

new elite at the expense others less well informed.

The use of a "social wage" will be imperative if a nonworking portion of society is going to be a part of the consumer population needed to purchase the goods that are made. The idea is illustrated in an exchange between the president of General Motors and Walter Reuther of the Auto-Workers' Trade Union. The GM executive "threatened to automate the entire factory and so expel all Reuther's members, declaring that 'Robots don't pay union dues.' To which came Reuther's famous reply,'But will robots buy your motor cars?' "[16]

There is nothing very revolutionary in the notion of people having money without having done much to earn it. Those with inherited wealth have long enjoyed this experience, and many people have benefited from scholarship grants and social security benefits enabling them to study or live without working. Then, too, there is the way in which some surgeons and doctors collect money through our health insurance system. The difference between what insurance pays for and the doctor's fee can be more than the entire surgery cost twenty years ago.

Anytime someone receives money without having to work for it, that money is a gift, a monetary equivalent of grace. As various techno-casualties begin to mount, becoming as some say the central social issue in America, Europe, and even Japan, the parable of the vineyard owner may become one of the more relevant and motivating passages in Holy Writ. God's work ethic has an exciting relevance both for today and for tomorrow.

The Center of Life

There may be a temptation to say that grace cannot be a work ethic or an ethic at all, or to say that this leads back to a two-kingdom separation. Grace is a gift that comes to us from God, one that conveys a perspective on how we understand and believe in God. An ethic, on the other hand, involves something we are to do, not just something we think or believe.

Grace does not cease being grace when it enters the workplace or when it is consciously shared. The name may change to "ethic." We may describe it as the "endurance of injustice" or "a new image of the working person." We may even feel a pressure to respond. However, the dynamic that is at work is still God and unmerited favor.

God is constantly giving new life, and this is God's gracious work, a sign of redemption. The receiving of grace is not limited to one hour a week in church on Sunday. In God we live and move and have our being all week long. Where grace is, God is. There is no grace apart from God and no God apart from grace. What God gives on Sunday through Word and sacrament is faith awareness and reinforcement of what God gives all week.

Thus, there are not two spheres, God's and the world's, but one reality, "encompassed, seized and possessed" by God.[17] God is not a religious being on the outside of life looking in at the end of a prayer chain. Instead, God is at the center of life right now.[18] This is not to suggest that everyone is aware of this or needs to be aware of this in order to function. As H. Richard Niebuhr once put it, "A genuinely disinterested science may be one of the greatest affirmations of faith and all the greater because it is so unconscious of what it is doing in this way."[19]

The grace of God is at the center of life whether or not we know it. Like the sun or rain, it falls on the just and the unjust. (See Matthew 5:45.) Thus, the center of life is unconscious. It belongs to the "depths." It is out of sight and out of mind, perceived only by faith. God's transcendence includes being at work within us but below our level of awareness. It is as if a "line" were drawn between our consciousness and God. The life of God is not given us to reflect upon. "I am not there with him. I am here with myself."[20] We may be aware of being inspired, but we are not aware of the source of our inspiration. Our primary consciousness is that we are inspired.

For us to perceive God immediately, the "ground," as it were, would have to be removed from under us. God would have to detach from us in order to approach our conscious awareness, and to do this God would have to become less than the One in whom we live, move, and have our being. To say that we cannot consciously perceive God or reach God is one thing, but to say that God cannot immediately perceive or communicate with us in understandable terms is quite another. The "detachment from us" is the God we know in Jesus Christ. Jesus is God's conscious approach to us, communicating with us in terms we can understand and in a form we can see.

There is one more point to be made. We cannot make grace the center of daily work. This would be like our trying to plant an oasis in a desert. The oasis is already there. Grace is already at the center. Even those steeped in a merit-oriented work ethic are alive by grace alone. Their first response is to recognize that what they may think is the center is not really the center at all. We may respond to the grace of God and the Word concerning it, but it is a response to what we have already received. We can share it, but we cannot achieve it.

Conversation Starters

The grace of God known as forgiveness is present in such forms as compassion, understanding, reinforcement, and encouragement. Do you agree or disagree? Why?

Is there a connection between the phrase "time heals" and the grace of God?

In the parable of the vineyard owner is Jesus relating grace to unemployment in the first century A.D.?

Capitalism is really cashing in on the grace of God. Do you agree or disagree? Why?

Allowing room for failure is implicit in shared decision making. Do you agree or disagree? Why?

Grace comes through Word and sacrament more than through the support of friends and co-workers. Do you agree or disagree? Why?

How can grace contain both demand and deliverance?

Automation renders the old work ethic passé for many people. Do you agree or disagree? Why?

Is there a difference between the grace proclaimed on Sunday and the new life God gives during the week?

If God's part in life is below our conscious level, how do we know that God is at work there?

Chapter 7

Daily Work
and the Arriving Kingdom

Does the work to build the earthly city, which is done by nine-tenths of humanity during nine-tenths of their time on earth, have any meaning in relation to the kingdom of God? This question was first asked by Teilhard de Chardin, a nineteenth century theologian/paleontologist.[1] A response to it engages us in this chapter.

What meaning exists depends in part on which priorities govern the building of the earthly city (a metaphor for society) and in part on how the kingdom of God is perceived. The church has traditionally seen the kingdom as a heavenly arrangement that bypasses earth. In the context of that perception, work here has been seen either as the price of admission or as an irrelevant factor. In the sixteenth-century Reformation neither work nor works counted for anything when it came to "getting into" heaven.

Jesus once said to Pontius Pilate: "My kingdom is not of this world" (John 18:36). This declaration calls for interpretation, and there is more than one possibility. This statement could be referring to either the destination or the origin of the kingdom. The petition in the Lord's Prayer, wherein Jesus prayed, "Thy kingdom come, thy will be done on earth as it is in heaven," requires no interpretation. In this prayer, Jesus affirmed that the kingdom of God is here, not just in the hereafter. And when the kingdom includes what happens here on earth, its relation to the building of the earthly city does have meaning. Then the kingdom shapes the priorities of our daily work.

The Genetic Lottery and Equal Opportunity

When the kingdom of God is related to daily work, it brings with it one of the most dynamic subjects in our time, namely, equality. There are different ways of talking about equality, the one best known by Americans being "equal opportunity," and the claim of many companies to be "equal opportunity employers." The reality, however, is that equal opportunity is a myth. There is no such thing, either at the starting line of a one-hundred-meter dash or in the workplace, because the conditions that are necessary for equal opportunity are not present.

When runners line up for a race, it might seem that the opportunity is the same for each of them. After all, the distance from start to finish is the same. However, the runners are not necessarily equal in ability or desire, and those factors will determine the outcome. Unless some differences exist, the race would never end. No one would win.

When several people are interviewed for one job, the personnel director has to eliminate all but one. This requires looking for certain qualities. It calls for criteria by which to weigh the applicants, and these criteria can be the previous work experience of the applicant or such qualities as sex, race, or personality. While conditions both before and after birth can contribute to inequality, it is the innate qualities that play the biggest part in making opportunity unequal. As infants we are all helpless at birth. Throughout life we all must eat and sleep, and if we are cut, we all will bleed. However, the conditions that lead to inequality are present before we enter the human race. They are present in the genes.

In his book *The Ethic of Democratic Capitalism*, Robert Benne slips in one sentence that alludes to this. It occurs near the end, but the content and scope of this one sentence is such that it really is *the* theological issue. If he tried to make it inconspicuous, he failed. It stands out like a sore thumb waiting to be treated. "Inequality results from the difference in the extent of talents given out in the natural lottery."[2]

The phrase "natural lottery" is another way of saying that God lets the genes determine the distribution of talents and intelligence, though Benne shies away from making that connection. By leaving it up to chance, the Creator is thereby freed from the charge of playing favorites. What this means is that God does not exercise personal supervision over who gets what talents and intelligence. Having set that process in motion, God allows it to play itself out according to what biologists call "genetic laws."

This does introduce into our understanding the idea of divine impartiality rather than divine favoritism. However, it fails to provide an equalizing principle by which we can understand God as a just God, for even if we speak of a "natural lottery" the Creator is still ultimately responsible. We may have depersonalized the selection process, but God is still responsible for having set the process in motion in the beginning. We will respond to this concern in the last section of this chapter. Here we acknowledge its validity.

Painful awareness of the inequality of opportunity and the conditions that contribute to it has moved some to call for equality of rewards, not just equality of opportunity. They do not see the conditions or the opportunities ever becoming truly even. The deeper issue—creation—stands in the way. One can appreciate their concern. In America the income difference between management and labor in business and industry is thirty to one. In hospital work it is ten to one, and in a university setting it is five to one.[3] Putting this another way, the bottom 20 percent of our citizens spend 79 percent of their income for food and fuel. The top 20 percent, on the other hand, spend only 20 percent for food and fuel, leaving them much more income to spend for housing, travel, transportation, and investments.[4]

What American has not strolled through a shopping mall and become aware of the many things one can buy at varied prices? Regardless of the item one might be shopping for—clothes, toys, sporting goods, jewelry or food—a common sight is their availability at different price levels. Inexpensive products exist, but they fall apart more quickly; durable products cost

more but are affordable primarily by those with higher incomes.
A shopping mall is a microcosm of the inequality in our society
and in the world.

The Climate for the Kingdom

If one were to gauge the climate for the kingdom on the basis
of letters to the editors of some mainline religious periodicals,
it would have to be a negative one. Then, too, there is the well-
publicized conservative mood of the country. One academician
who felt conservatives were being underestimated said, "Just
wait until the implications sink into lay minds." He was referring
to the tendency of mainline church leaders to blame North
American affluence for poverty conditions in Latin America. He
was predicting stormy weather for those churches.

The editor of *The Lutheran* wrote to me that hostile letters
represent but 2½ percent of the church membership. Unfortunately, the people who shout are often those who are heard.
Many pastors have shied away from speaking out lest they
offend someone. One wonders what would happen if mainline
church people had the opportunity to respond to an issue and
then let the "implications sink in." What would happen when
the truth hit the fan? Would all hell break loose, or what?

We ask this because we wish to share such an experience
and the results from mainline church folks who responded to
it. The results were intriguing. (This is an activity that any
congregation could use in testing their own climate for the arriving kingdom.)

The activity gave the participants written descriptions of two
different ways people might relate to one another in society.
Both ways were presented in the context of belief in God. One
way reflects a belief in inequality while the other suggests a
belief in equality of some kind. The two ways were placed side
by side so that the readers could compare them more easily.

After reading the two descriptions, participants were asked
to read over a list of twenty items and indicate for each item
whether it could be expected to show up in Society 1 or Society
2. The reason for this was to see if there might be any grouping
or coalescing of the items in relation to each society. Might the
items have some connections with each other and with the

Society 1	Society 2
This society assumes that it is the Creator's will that the needs of all people be met, but not equally. The work of some citizens is to be regarded as of more worth to the community than is the work of others. Each person, therefore, is rewarded for his or her work in proportion to the value of the service performed. The result is different levels of income permitting the purchase of goods and services at varying prices.	This society assumes that it is the Creator's will to meet the minimum needs of all people equally despite differences in color, IQ, and talent. This society further assumes that each person performs a function that is indispensable to the life of the community and so monetary compensation is fairly even. Because income levels are similar, the goods, services, and neighborhoods are also fairly equal in cost and quality.

society prompting their selection? It is readily acknowledged that the items had connections in the mind of the person who wrote the question, but would these connections also exist in the thinking of mainline church folks?

A chart of the results lists the items and shows how they coalesced in the thinking of participants. The items on the survey forms were, of course, mixed together. In order to make comparison easier, they are presented in rank order of their percent of response.

It would seem from these percentages that people were in substantial agreement on where to place the items; the connections did not exist only in the mind of the writer. The participants were describing two societies, one that fosters economic inequality and one that strives for some kind of economic equality. Then, too, since all the items were drawn from our culture (from literature or conversation), there would appear to be two different and conflicting sets of priorities and effects in America. Of course, when grouped in the table found on page 106, the connections seem logical, almost common sense. However, it must be remembered that on the survey form the items were mixed together.

Society 1	
(inequality and its effects)	
Climbing a social ladder	96%
A drive to be number one	93
Getting ahead at other's expense	93
Keeping up with the Joneses	93
Profiting from genetic differences	92
Home burglary systems	91
Hostility between income groups	91
Winners and losers	88
Welfare programs	80
Meeting a challenge	70

Society 2	
(equality and its effects)	
Looking out for each other	84%
Lower "mountains," fill in "valleys"	84
Mutual support and gratitude	83
Mutual respect and trust	82
Liberty and justice for all	81
Fulfilling creation	71
A sense of interdependence	69
Rapport between labor and management	68
A sense of calling	64

When the logic inherent in the two societies is articulated, we find that the middle-income persons' hue and cry about welfare is directly related to a society that fosters inequality and not to a society that seeks to make the economic ground more even. Also, genetic differences were acknowledged by respondents, but profiting from such differences was clearly placed in a society that fosters inequality. It is further apparent that the "Creator's will" received a kind of definition in each society by the coalescing of the items. "Fulfilling creation" and "a sense of calling" are phrases that have theological connotations, and both were associated with the equality-oriented society.

The underlying dynamics of care, support, rapport, and trust were apparently considered by the participants to be part of the society seeking some kind of equality. They reflect a work ethic based on grace. They contribute to the arriving kingdom and they reveal some of the fruits of the Spirit that Paul wrote about in Galatians 5. On the other hand, dynamics related to inequality were envy, fear, pride, anger, and greed; each of these is one of the "deadly sins" to which Scripture points.[5]

However, before we draw any conclusions concerning the climate for the arriving kingdom, we must share what happens when the "implications sink in." This moment of truth occurred in the second part of the activity. In part 2 the respondents were to look at the two societies and decide in which one they would prefer to live. Here the response becomes disconcerting and intriguing, for here we catch a glimpse of our receptivity and lack of receptivity to the kingdom we pray for with regularity.

Although respondents had revealed substantial agreement in making the connections in part one of the activity, when it came to choosing the society in which they would prefer to live, they parted company and moved away from each other. It was like a parade coming to an intersection where some of the marchers turned left while others turned right. Sixty percent preferred living in a society striving for equality, where the priorities of God's kingdom would be at work. Forty percent, on the other hand, preferred to live in a society based on inequality, where traits of human nature abounded. The division cut across occupational lines but occurred more evenly in some occupations than in others. Teachers, homemakers, secretaries, and doctors tended to prefer equality to inequality, whereas those from the business and sales fields and from the trades were divided fifty-fifty.

We should bear in mind that these people were from the middle or upper-middle income level in the church. It would be easy to assume that folks who live in the suburbs, have nice homes and pleasant neighborhoods—as was true in this case— would be somewhat unified in their thinking about the system that makes their socio-economic privileges possible. We might believe them to be highly satisfied and unreceptive to any thought of disrupting the hand that feeds them. The clues that emerged in their responses to this question, however, indicate that the majority who responded to it are receptive to a more just world, one where the distribution of goods and services is more equal, one where a work ethic based on grace is operational. At the same time, the 40 percent (those who preferred inequality, or

Society 1) is much higher than *The Lutheran* editor's 2½ percent. One can't help but wonder what is going on here. The fact that the people who participated were among the "seeking" members of their congregations—many were enrolled in adult education groups—is offset by the fact that something more basic than seeking was touched in part two of the activity. One may wonder what they are seeking.

Why Some Turn Left and Others Turn Right

Some might say that equality is the "right" answer, that those who preferred inequality were more honest, less pressured to say what they thought the church wanted to hear. It is true that the 40 percent reveal honesty, but do we have the right to apply a different standard to the 60 percent?

What we can suggest is that both groups might have been responding to some personal experience, not just to words on paper. Members from both groups have done well in an economic system that fosters inequality. They have been the winners not the losers. They have profited from genetic differences. They have successfully climbed the social ladder or are doing so. If equality sounded like the end of all these benefits to some, it may have been that inequality sounded like the end of these benefits to others. Most of the participants over forty years of age probably remembered the days when the doors to their homes could be left unlocked. Today, even for those living in the suburbs, there is a heightened awareness of crime. People in both urban and suburban neighborhoods often band together and take turns driving around looking for strange cars or individuals. Home security has become big business.

Linking home burglary systems to the society based on inequality would seem to suggest an awareness of this reality and could very easily have prompted many to prefer a better, safer place to live, which more equality in the society would encourage. Why some would still prefer the insecurity of inequality is puzzling. It reinforces the thought that there is something deeper at work here, and we may have a clue as to what that is.

Thanks to the capacity of the computer to remember the responses of those who participated in a study, it was possible to compare a person's response to one question with that same person's response to other questions. This provides relevant insight into why some turned left and others turned right. What this tells us is that neither the 40 percent (Society 1) nor the 60 percent (Society 2) made their decision on the basis of impulse or in response to outside pressure alone. Responses were made on the basis of personal faith and commitment to different values and priorities.

For example, it was learned from those who prefer a society based on inequality that they also:

- consider God more concerned with spiritual needs than with material needs.
- are more inclined to value independence from the claims of God.
- resent the way inflation cuts into the results of their hard work.
- are more inclined to see poverty as something communism exploits.

On the other hand, it was discovered that those who prefer a society in search of equality also:

- are more inclined to see God's goal to be that of balancing privileges.
- are more aware of the Good News when they are in church and realize that they hunger for it.
- are more troubled by hearing profanity in their daily work-places.
- are inclined to find new truth more therapeutic than threat- ening.

It would appear that among church members who prefer a society based on *inequality* there is a greater commitment to the Protestant work ethic. God has a place in their faith, but it is one that allows the "believer" the freedom to move about in the pursuit of material goods and to choose the ways they are obtained. They go to church, pray the prayers, sing the songs, and hear the sermons on Sunday, but on Monday when they return to the workplace another standard becomes operative.

Moreover, the church members who make up the 40 percent (those who chose Society 1) sense a gap between their beliefs and the real world which they do not believe can be bridged. They feel that they must make peace with reality and that reality does not allow much room for the incarnation of the values of faith in any practical sense. Indeed, the intrusion of faith into daily life disturbs the equilibrium they have achieved in the methods and aims of daily work.

One man even articulated this in the following words he wrote alongside the questions we have been discussing:

> I chose Society 1 because in your Society 2 you are suggesting an ideal situation, i.e., a kind of utopia (in religious terms—the kingdom of God). Responses are obvious caricatures and bear no resemblance to the difficulty of having to live in a condition where the kingdom is present but not yet.

Neither equality nor the kingdom are viable options in this world for one who thinks this way. In view of the emerging rapport between management and labor, one would have to say that neither is Reformation II a viable option. However, if an underprivileged person says that a more equitable distribution of goods and service is "ideal," that is one thing. When a privileged person says it, that is something else. If a person chooses inequality because it is more "real," it would seem that he or she does not want to be made aware of an alternative that is more equitable; the elephant is once again dancing among the chickens. Architects and city planners use drawing boards all the time to design cities and buildings. Why could we not do the same to make life more safe and secure for all the people who are going to live and work in these cities and buildings?

Church members who comprise the 60 percent (those who chose Society 2), on the other hand, seem to have room in their faith for an appreciation of God's unmerited grace. They are sensitive to the need for a greater balance of the material privileges that presently divide the world into such uneven realms. They, too, are aware of the differences between Sunday and Monday, but this is not a difference they feel God wants. They, too, have been brought up on the Protestant work ethic. However, they believe that God desires to share the wealth with everybody. A new work ethic is taking shape within them.

What we also have here is an example of how fear of communism can blind someone to the social justice and grace priorities God sets forth in Scripture. The 40 percent were very apprehensive about communism; also two respondents scribbled the words "communist" or "socialist" in the margin beside the description of a society seeking more equality. Many of us have been brought up to think that communism's number one transgression is atheism. The reaction of these two respondents, however, reveals that for them the real "sin" is not to deny belief in God, but to affirm belief in equality. The reader will recall that both societies were presented in the context of the Creator's will. To ignore this and concentrate instead on the equality factor tells what these two persons consider important. "God" is not the real issue. Economic status is.

It would seem reasonable to conclude that the climate for the arriving kingdom is good among the 60 percent. As far as the 40 percent is concerned, they do seem to recognize the difference between the effects of equality and inequality. They have the vision even if they lack the commitment to change. Perhaps when the circumstances are favorable or they have the opportunity to discuss these issues with others in the congregation, a revised view will emerge. "The prophets . . . were sent to those who acknowledged at least verbally, even if not actually, the same covenant and law as they did."[6]

Grain and Missiles in the Global City

Even if the climate for the arriving kingdom among 60 percent of the members of one church body may represent a much wider mainline constituency, it still occurs within the confines of the United States. Because the kingdom is God's, we must take into account all life on this planet. There are many tongues spoken, but there is one God who speaks them all fluently.

Because the kingdom is God's, nationalism must give way to internationalism, and equality in one country is but one piece in the big picture. Moreover, because the kingdom is a place in the world and not in a church building, we find ourselves lifting up the connections that have already made this world seem smaller. Just as trucks carry products across town, so freighters carry such products across oceans. Just as subways and cars carry workers from their homes to their places of employment, so planes transport business persons from cities to other continents. Thanks to a network of telephone cables connecting continents, it is even possible to think that we could have yellow pages identifying global services, and a business person in Nigeria saying to one in Boston, "Why didn't you call?"

It is especially appropriate in a theology of work to think of the relationship between worldwide work and the arriving kingdom because daily work either plays a key part in achieving the priorities of that kingdom or blocks its arrival. Although there is ample reason for speaking of a military-industrial complex, there is also reason for calling attention to a difference in the contribution that kinds of work make to the coming kingdom.

Work in one part of the global city can bring food to people in another part. Some work brings raw materials from places that have them to places that lack them. Transnational corporations, despite their exploitation of cheap labor, do transfer some of the wealth of the rich to the poor, wealth that was not there before. And if Reformation II continues, even that may increase. It is estimated that, by the year 2000, approximately 30 percent of all manufacturing will take place in the so-called developing countries, where the work force can produce goods for less.[7] We say "so-called" because the present industry-oriented parts of the city, which are shifting to computerized, information/service fields of work, also appear to be developing.

Cheaper labor costs in other countries have led to the relocation of a number of American companies there and to the "dumping" of less expensive goods on our markets. However, the resulting unemployment we are experiencing here is a kind of turnabout for what many of the poor in other lands have known all their lives. When Scripture speaks about lowering mountains and raising valleys, the message now has an intercontinental scope as well as a national or local one. Since the kingdom is the Creator's, it can come only as the misery and poverty in all parts of the world are relieved, making the rough places more even. This can occur only if the economic forces at work in the world continue to encourage nations to reach out for foreign markets as imports and exports between countries cross each other on the high seas.

The grain sales to Russia probably do more for the cause of peace and the deterrence of nuclear war than all the missiles presently owned and being built by both countries. In a way we are doing what Jesus said to do—feeding our enemies. A country such as Russia, which is in need of food, is going to think twice about destroying the hand that feeds its people.

There is both irony and tragedy in the preoccupation of the

superpowers with military defense. While they speak of deterrence, of making enough missiles so that to start a war would be suicide, anyone knows that you cannot kill someone more than once. The stockpiles of missiles are unnecessary. They are redundant. They do not serve a military purpose. However, they do serve an economic one, and this is the irony and the tragedy. The irony is that one billion dollars spent on missile production will supply an estimated 30,000 jobs,[8] but the tragedy is that the product is of such explosive danger that the workers may not live to spend their income.

The efforts that communism and capitalism expend to contain each other are counterproductive. Such efforts not only create insecurity throughout the global city, but they put workers in opposition to the arriving kingdom with every day's pay they draw. Fear does not lead to security but to insecurity, whether the city is a national or global one. Such insecurity has no place in the kingdom of God. Only trust fits there, and trust comes from people who are getting to know one another and who are working for a common cause.

God's arriving kingdom contains that trust and that purpose. If we really believe that the United States is a Christian nation, or the "good guys," and Russia is an atheistic one, or the "bad guys," then it is only from us that the initiative can come that will penetrate the wall of hostility between us. There is much incentive for peacemakers in the arriving kingdom.

God has already demonstrated in Jesus Christ the unilateral decision to bring aid and comfort to enemies. Jesus' visible ministry on earth was in the midst of people who were extremely hostile toward one another. The situation in his day was much like the one today between the United States and other parts of the world. Rome was the affluent party getting rich from the taxes levied on its conquered provinces. The Jews had no more love for Pilate than poor people in Latin America have for Ronald Reagan. It was into that hornet's nest that Jesus was born and raised. It was to that smoldering caldron of hate that he came with goodwill, causing one Roman centurian to say, "Just say the word, Lord, and I know that my servant will be healed," and another soldier to exclaim "Truly this was the Son of God." (See Luke 7:7 and Matthew 27:54.)

Jesus saw clearly that through compassion and reconciliation

God's peace could come on earth. He also saw that someone had to initiate it. He did not see the "things that make for peace" as utopian or demonic; he saw peace as a sign of God's kingdom, the way God works. Jesus had complete trust in the pursuit of peace and reconciliation as God's way, even to the point of dying for it on the cross. And God revealed support of Jesus' faith by raising him from the dead. It is highly unlikely that God intended Jesus' followers to embark on a military course.

Caution: God at Work

Although, as Creator, God is responsible for setting the genetic lottery in motion, the witness of Scripture is that God is at work to redeem humanity from the effects of inequality. God is the hidden pressure for equality and the arriving kingdom. We must be careful in speaking about "men at work" as if no other being or power is involved.

God's interest in equality first appears in the thinking of the Hebrew prophet Ezekiel, who declares on two occasions that God's ways are equal, whereas those of Israel are not (Ezekiel 18:25-29, KJV).

In the New Testament the question of God's relation to equality surfaces at several points. In the *Good News Bible*, the Bible in Today's English Version, Acts 10:34 reads, "God treats everyone on the same basis," and in Ephesians 6:9 and 1 Peter 1:17 the words are that God judges all people "by the same standard." One of the implicit messages in such words is that saying them would not have been necessary if people had already been thinking of God that way. We see this background in a first-century congregation where inequality was rearing its uneven head. Observing that well-dressed visitors were made to feel more welcome than poorly dressed ones, James stated that partiality is unbecoming to those who "hold the faith of our Lord Jesus Christ." (See James 2:1-7.) The term "impartiality" may sound like neutrality, as may the thought of God judging everyone by the same standard. However, in a situation where people are divided into social classes, sides have already been established, and the concept of impartiality is anything but neutral. It introduces a new dimension, one that can be activated only by being partial to impartiality.

In Jesus' life and ministry, Jesus placed himself squarely on the side of those left out or looked down upon as sinful or inferior—people with perhaps few talents. His parable of the talents almost seems out of character compared with his everyday activity and the story about the vineyard owner.

This accent on equality puts contemporary meaning into the thought that there is no foundation other than the one we have in Jesus Christ.[9] Jesus pointed to the importance of a foundation in his parable about the two houses—one built on rock, the other on sand—and how the storms of life destroyed one but not the other. (See Matthew 7:24-27 or Luke 6:46-49.) It would be a mistake to think that Jesus was only thinking of a private relationship to God when he told this parable. It pertains to communities and society as well. We cannot use a "rock foundation" in our personal life and faith and "sand foundation" as the basis for society without running into serious trouble.

This suggests that much depends on our response to what Jesus said, and to be sure, the story about the two houses begins with the words, "Whoever hears the words of mine and does them is like. . . ." However, this leads us to recognizing God at work not just "men at work." Since the foundation represents the priorities evident in the life and ministry of Jesus, we have here a foundation in which the Creator has a vested interest. Anyone who builds on that foundation, who seeks to lower the mountains of inequality, is going to find a source of strength working within, namely God Almighty.

When Jesus urged his friends to pray, "Thy kingdom come, thy will be done, on earth . . .," it was about as direct an invitation to God to act in society as one could utter. It applies to the church, but it did not originate in a church building. In his letters Paul wrote that we are a new creation in Christ. (See 2 Corinthians 5:17 and Galatians 6:15.) This can be true only if God is doing something redemptive *now*. Otherwise, the coming of God's kingdom would depend on us, and the present tense of Paul's statement would be meaningless.

In his second letter to the Corinthians Paul goes one step further. He speaks of grace in the context of equality in a way that links equality with Reformation II. When some congregations in Macedonia gave money to poor people in Judea, Paul perceived this as a reflection of their faith in Jesus who "though he was rich . . . became poor so that . . . you might become rich." This action Paul referred to as "grace." (See 2 Corinthians 8:1-14.) He implied that the Corinthians had a model here; but then as quickly as he implied this, he assured them that he was not suggesting that they simply trade places with those who were poor. He was suggesting generosity.

Paul saw equality working itself out over a period of time in the sense that those who give now may need to receive at a later date. Actually, equality does not result in the "haves" and "have nots" trading places. It results in the lopsidedness of the world being evened off so that all have enough.

Robert Lekachman, Professor of Economics at Lehman College, City University of New York, writes that in the greed of the rich is located the salvation of the poor.[10] Were we to amend his thought to take faith into account, it might read: "Only in the grace and equality of Jesus Christ does the greed of the rich become the economic salvation of the poor."

Conversation Starters

The kingdom of God refers to a heavenly place apart from a time or place on earth. Do you agree or disagree? Why?

The conditions that lead to inequality are present in the genes. Do you agree or disagree? Why?

What does the presence of two societal foundations in America say?

Why do some prefer equality and others prefer inequality?

Is communism's chief sin its atheism or its interest in equality?

Grain sales to Russia can do more for world security than the stockpiling of missiles can. Do you agree or disagree? Why?

God is at work to redeem humanity from the effects of inequality. Do you agree or disagree? Why?

We cannot build a personal faith on a rock foundation and build the philosophy of our society on sand. Do you agree or disagree? Why?

Chapter 8

Toward a
Daily-Work-Oriented Church

That's an odd title in a way. Most of the people who comprise the church are also members of the nation's work force and have been for much of their lives. For many worshipers their daily work is a part of them when they show up for church on Sunday. So how can we talk about moving toward what already is? Because for so long the church has not expressed concern for people in the work world, for it to articulate such concern is like suggesting something new. Thus, what this title and this chapter are doing is celebrating the obvious. The longstanding silence in church relating to the priorities of daily work is over. Indeed, if the reader is a church member, that silence was broken on page 1.

Given the number of church members who participate in some form of daily work, the theme of this chapter is an inclusive one. It not only includes the growing number of women who work outside the home, but it also includes minorities. It includes all who are employed or who would like to be. Daily work is a human bond. It is also a source of socio-economic division, and it is time to bridge this gap.

The church is a natural place to make the connections between the gospel and weekday work, and not just because of the laity. As one midwestern theological school professor said concerning the clue search report: "This report should challenge the full range of church experiences—from pastors and congregations to bishops to national divisions and offices." What is at stake is the Good News of the kingdom that shapes the church's message and purpose. The way grace and daily work are involved in the arriving kingdom intensifies the power and relevancy of this theme.

What follows are some steps toward a daily-work-oriented church. They can be initiated by lay persons or clergy. And while they may seem like small steps for either initiator, they are steps that can reinforce the reformation in the workplace and provide a new dimension to the one in the church.

Raising the Subject

Breaking the sound barrier calls for a combination of the right questions and a willingness to listen and to let others respond. It is E.F. Hutton in reverse. When E.F. Hutton (an "authority") listens, everybody talks . . . though hopefully not all at the same time. This can occur in forums, committees, boards, councils, and in adult classes. Robert Raines, author of *New Life in the Church*, says that in the beginning of his ministry he felt compelled to "prime the pump" if he was going to get people to talk. What brought new life to his congregation was the discovery that all he had to do was to share a question or a brief statement and then let people share what they thought about it.

Some appropriate questions might be "What signs of change in managerial style are showing up at work these days?" or "What evidence is there of workers being given more of a voice in decisions that affect them?" Such questions might be especially appropos in congregations composed of middle-income or management persons.

When there are no signs or evidence of change in the workplace, the subject can be opened up by utilizing the questions in this book. There is much incentive in the way participants in the clue search responded to the opportunity to talk about faith and daily work.

A few were threatened by the effort to relate grace and the workplace. One person wrote in the evaluation of the discussion that his group "sort of backed off from the entire subject," and another wrote that one couple dropped out because "they were threatened." However, I believe it was Emerson who said that God offers to every mind its choice between truth and repose, and the overwhelming majority of participants found both in the combination of questions and discussion. The group that backed off the subject followed the lead of one lay person who held the group in his sway.

The strongest evidence of the receptivity of people to these kinds of issues emerged in the length of time groups spent discussing them. As research investigators, we had assumed that four weeks would be sufficient to discuss the search, and we noted this in a cover letter. This was the amount of time normally given to research responses. However, when four weeks had passed and only two groups had reported, we began to wonder what was happening. We discovered that people became so engrossed in sharing their thoughts on this subject with one another that weeks went by before they were ready to send in the completed forms. Several groups reported that after spending six weeks, they had "barely scratched the surface." Another spoke of spending three months. One group apologized for taking so much time, explaining, "We found we could get through only about one question per Sunday morning." Since there were thirty-two questions in the search, this meant that their forum planned to spend eight months on the subject of daily work. Truly they were moving toward a daily-work-oriented church.

There are words of added encouragement for the church in the response of these people. One response was that they enjoyed sharing reactions to questions in a questionnaire. Another, inseparable from the first, was that they enjoyed sharing reactions to these particular questions. One group said, "The questions are excellent for discussion." Another reporter stated why they were excellent for discussion: "Our people are finding it extremely helpful and very relevant for their everyday lives." In other words, the excellence was in the subject matter, subject matter that was already within the participants, just waiting to be released.

Still another word lurking behind the scenes here is that lay people have thoughts to share and many respond quickly when given the opportunity to do so in small groups. Adult education programs in many churches put into the hands of participants books called "pupils books," a term that conveys an image of ignorance. The books may raise some subjects for discussion but only after the "pupils" have read a number of paragraphs or a chapter in their books. The written material is like a sermon on paper or like several sermons back to back. The response to discussing the clue search questions indicates that we do not need lengthy input in order to respond; we just need the chance, the green light. It is for this reason that statements and questions for discussion appear at the end of each chapter in this book.

Identifying Grace in Daily Work

The identification of grace will emerge in the above settings. However, it is also important that lay people realize that the pastoral leadership in the congregation is supporting them in the move toward a daily-work-oriented church. This support should occur in relation to both the message and the medium in which it is conveyed. The two are intimately related.

In the sixteenth century the sermon moved the grace of God from the altar to the pulpit, or about thirty feet closer to the pews. The accent on the sermon was an improvement both in content and in geography. Over the years, however, the medium came to convey a message of its own; the preacher was the authority, the one to be listened to. Today that message is quietly shouting at people while the person in the pulpit seeks to communicate the Word of God.

In moving toward a daily-work-oriented church, the preacher will want to distinguish between the psuedo grace of the Protestant work ethic and the genuine grace of God, both of which are present in Scripture. At the same time, he or she will also want contemporary illustrations of grace to come from the workplace as well as from Scripture. And for such illustrations there is no better source than the people in the pews. They are the biblical commentary once the exegetical work has been done. The pastor, if honest, is the recognized amateur when it comes to being a source for such illustrations. The real pros are in the pews.

Meeting with people where they work is one positive way of obtaining such insight. However, since most of the folks in the pews are in the workplace all week, every week, the same thing can be accomplished by asking a few of them at a time to meet to share their thoughts on an upcoming sermon text, to help make the connection between grace and daily work. In fact, every sermon begins the moment the preacher starts to think about what to preach, or how to approach a particular text. Similarly, the sermon would begin in such meetings with lay people. Lay persons could provide the experience and the theologically trained member could provide some interpretation possibilities to be tested with the lay people present.

Having met with them, the preacher would continue the sermon from the pulpit. Everybody in the congregation assembled on that day would hear the pastor make the connection between God, grace, the arriving kingdom, and the workplace where they spend so much of their God-given time Monday through Friday. When the person in the pew hears the person in the pulpit describe the way it actually is "out there," this realism becomes a form of grace that is communicated. Such thoughts produce a silent echo in the ears of the pew sitter and a response like, "Hey, the pastor knows me. She or he understands what daily work is like for me." Indeed, there is more to grace than a five-minute conclusion to a sermon that spends fifteen minutes on how we are to live as Christians in daily life.

Listeners who have been accustomed to transferring words about grace into something they are to be or do would, perhaps for the first time, not be able to do this. They would not be able to do anything except say yes in their minds. Sin is built into the economic system, and there is no way to escape it except personally to become aware of the grace of God at work.

Those whose participation in church life reminds them of the large gap between grace and daily work would hear through such thoughts from the pulpit that the workplace is "owned" by God's servants; the chasm is being bridged. The God of grace is truly "speaking" through the ordained spokesperson. God is truly at the center of life.

A group of national church staff persons gathered for a conference on the theme "Born Anew to Serve." Preconference information noted that one speaker was an authority on how to motivate volunteers in the church, and another speaker, a theological professor, was going to focus on "Baptism and Servanthood." The announced agenda seemed like an unofficial performance review. It sounded as if the emphasis was going to be on "trying harder." To those who were already over-extended, this was not exactly good news. The first three speakers, however, were fellow staff members who had been asked to share their expectations for the conference. What two of them shared was filled with the dynamic of grace, though neither of them used that term. Ironically, what they said set a new work ethic in motion at the conference.

One of them said that as an editor he never saw the people he was serving. He said the last thing he wanted to hear for the next two days was the need to reach people. What he wanted to hear was how his work could be more meaningful. In front of the whole staff he acknowledged that it would be frustrating for him to be exhorted to more service.

The other staff member frankly admitted that in the sixties she was highly motivated to serve others above and beyond the call of duty. However, now in the eighties she did not feel that kind of motivation.

The first speaker said that his words were coming from "my unborn silent me," but in an atmosphere charged with the anticipation of being admonished to greater effort and dedication, his words came across like the grace of God. Rather than applying pressure, the words of the speakers relieved it. The result was that we all were motivated by grace to participate in the conference in a new way, with a new lease on life, a new feeling about our work.

Now if church staff people feel the burden of performance or the need to achieve, how much more keenly do those in the competitive arena of daily work feel this burden? Moreover, if church staff folks need grace, how much more do people whose daily work is in the trenches of business and industry, struggling with others for a slice of the economic pie, need grace? We can hardly improve on the experience of Paul, who in his letter to the Corinthians acknowledged that when he spoke of his weaknesses, his human frailty, his "unborn silent me," somehow the power of Christ joined his words and filled listeners with the grace of God. (See 2 Corinthians 12:6b-10.)

There is one more thing that must be said about the sermon as a means of support for a daily-work-oriented church. It is not possible for any one preacher to apply God's Word to the workplace of every person in the pews, given the variety of places wherein they work. One way to offset this source of frustration for the listener is for the pastor to structure the worship experience in such a way that part of the sermon time or postworship time is spent in "application groups." In such groups each listener would have the opportunity, in a small group setting, to share how the Word of grace relates to his or her daily work or to hear this from others. The groups could bring together people of similar occupational backgrounds or age. However, the conversation would build on whatever emerged in the initial sermon text discussion with other lay members. Such application opportunities would also be a part of the Word for the day, a part of the sermon.

Communing with the Carpenter

It was a unique service in that no words were spoken. None had to be. A mixture of familiar and new images did the talking. Little children were acting out the story of the Nativity. Smiles appeared on parental faces as offspring momentarily assumed the roles of Mary, Joseph, shepherds, and wisemen. The time was late fall. The incarnation was the call to worship.

Once the little children had finished, this service took an unprecedented turn. High school youth came down the side aisles to the front pew and stopped there. Each was dressed in the garb of a worker or professional person. Each carried something that worker would use to perform his or her task, a symbol of the workplace.

On cue the procession began. From alternating sides of the sanctuary, the youth walked to the chancel and laid their symbols on the altar. The garb and symbols had been chosen with care to represent the kinds of work that the adults sitting in the pews did during the week. The point was to provide an opportunity for identification in an atmosphere of reflection. A guitar was strummed softly in the background.

A carpenter dressed in blue overalls with the large pockets was first. He walked to the altar and placed a hammer on it.

Then from the other side a nurse moved to the altar with a wash basin and towel. Next, came a business executive carrying a brief case, and he was followed across the nave by an automobile mechanic dressed in dirty brown coveralls. He placed a can of motor oil on the altar. Soon a stethescope, an ax, an eraser, and a menu found their way to the sacred place as the procession continued with a doctor, a fireman, a school teacher, and a waitress. As each worker left the altar, he or she assumed a position in a semicircle facing it.

When all were in place, two young adults dressed in the first-century clothing of Mary and Joseph, walked down the center aisle carrying a loaf of bread and a bottle of wine. As they reached the altar area, they were greeted by a pastor who took the bread and wine and placed them also on the altar in a small space that had been left for that purpose. Slowly and quietly he lifted the bread and wine toward the cross above the altar and then proceeded to give each of the "workers" the elements.

When they had communed, they stepped to the sides of the chancel, then it was the congregation's turn. Although no words were spoken audibly, it is safe to assume that many thoughts were shared in silence as members of the church came forward to celebrate communion with the Carpenter, mindful that his or her daily work had also been blessed in some way by the Lord's presence.

This way of celebrating the obvious, done on an annual basis in a congregation, illustrates how the Eucharist can be a part of the new awareness within a daily-work-oriented church. It also highlights by contrast what was learned about participation in this sacrament by participants in the clue search project. The question had to do with what went on in the minds of people as they were in the process of communing. It was found that the words "given and shed *for you*" were personally meaningful. However, less than one out of three thought about a daily work concern during that personal moment. Had Jesus Christ been raised in a parsonage, as the son of a pastor and his or her spouse, this might be understandable. In view of the fact that Jesus, as a carpenter, was a member of the daily work force of the first century, it is disconcerting.

Literally speaking, only those today who work with wood could meaningfully bring their daily concerns with them to this experience. The other extreme is that Jesus Christ was so highly spiritualized that we do not think of him as knowing anything about the workplace. It is to offset this image that we have lifted up his occupation during the first thirty years of the Incarnation.

What is encouraging from the response to the clue search is that nearly half of the participants indicated that if the sermon touches something real in their lives, this goes with them to the altar and shapes their communion thoughts. This is encouraging because if the sermon does relate to the workplace, there is reason to expect that people will consciously realize the participation of the Lord in that time-consuming, energy-draining sphere of life. Word and sacrament would compliment each other here as a means of grace in a way that has not been a part of our experience in church up to now.

The Informal Sacrament

What is more related to the workplace is the informal conversation that occurs among church members.

Mark Gribbon, a researcher for the Alban Institute of Washington, D.C., was interviewing people in a congregation when he discovered that one of the favorite projects for men in the parish was to sell Christmas trees on a lot next to the church building. It was apparent that raising money was not the only motivation behind this project. So what was the incentive? What was going on?

He learned what it was in a roundabout way. He was asking people why they participated in the church when one of the men said, "It's less expensive than psychotherapy. You get a chance to talk with people and you discover that they have as hard a time with their daily work or with raising kids as you do." At this point Mark asked, "And where do these conversations take place?" The young man replied, "Oh, most anyplace, like when we sell Christmas trees."

In a prior chapter we spoke of the "mutual conversation and consolation of the brethren" as a Reformation description of an informal means by which the grace of God comes to us. It is relevant here to see that this process occurred while these men were acknowledging difficulties at work, and freely sharing their weaknesses, trouble, or other daily concerns.

There is more and more evidence that one of the most important places in the church building, for lay persons, is the narthex or vestibule, the zone just outside the door of the nave where socializing goes on. However, socializing can also take place wherever a cup of coffee is served on the premises. When some young adults who were participating in the life of the church (most were not) were asked what it was that attracted them, the most common response was that people were friendly and warm. Very few of them said it was because of the worship or sermon. None said that the sacraments drew them to the church.

This feeling of warmth and friendliness is shared when people are mixing and talking together, greeting one another after a week in the workplace. The worship service may be over or not yet begun, but the people are still assembled in the name of One who promised to be wherever such a gathering occurs. It might seem that much or even most of the conversation has little to do with the message proclaimed in the worship setting. However, it is nonetheless a product of the grace that binds the people together. Moreover, if the mutual consolation of the brothers and sisters is truly a channel for the grace of God, then we need to declare it as such so that members of the church might begin to know and appreciate what God is doing in their midst. It could very well be that one reason the conversation has little to do with the message proclaimed in the worship service is that the message has little to do with the conversation. There would seem to be a greater chance for such conversation to include the name of God if we in the church were to identify all of the places where the grace of God is at work.

Providing Support Groups

One other way laity and clergy can move toward a daily-work-oriented church is to establish support groups for that purpose. There are two groups of people today that could benefit from support. One is the group—perhaps the majority—whose workplace is still under the tyranny of merit and profit, where the impact of Reformation II has yet to be felt. The other is the group that is unemployed.

In situations in which a church member has nothing approaching a "quality circle" in his or her workplace, the church could provide a support group as a temporary substitute or as a source of inspiration. People from similar walks of life or the same corporation could meet to share concerns that weigh upon them. Inasmuch as these would take place in a congregation that is moving toward a daily-work orientation, the subjects or issues discussed would draw upon a variety of sources within the fellowship. Some subjects might be rather technical, problem-solving concerns that would make work more effective or easier. This could include a pooling of ideas from which their companies could benefit as well. As management persons perceive such employees becoming a reservoir of ideas, the source might be shared; the relevance of the church and the value of quality circles might be introduced or more appreciated.

Other subjects or issues discussed could have more to do with the morale of workers in places where they have no voice in decisions or no share in the profits. Since the insensitivity of management to the helpful insights and the human needs of workers is a major source of low morale, understanding managerial persons would be helpful. Fortunately, greater understanding is available today because of our new awareness of the brain's division into right and left sides and the implications of the fact that human beings usually have an orientation toward one side or the other. Left-brained persons are inclined toward hierarchical authority and carefully planned situations. They tend to base decisions on data and analysis. They strive to preserve traditional assumptions about people and economic activity. Right-brained persons are inclined toward participatory authority, spontaneity, intuition, and feelings. They like to brainstorm and to challenge traditional assumptions.[1] Thus, the difference may have more to do with genetics than with personal preferences, and our ability to understand and accept this difference is enhanced. We see the workplace turning somewhat toward right-brain orientation. In the interests of self-understanding, knowledge of the two orientations is both relevant and important if left-brain-oriented individuals are going to accept themselves and be more open to the needs of the present and the future.

Unemployed people need material as well as spiritual support. Immediate needs may be for food and shelter, and some congregations are seeking to provide both. A local food-shelf group in Omaha made a filmstrip that was effective in convincing grocers and food producers in the area that it would be better to give excess food to the food shelf than to haul it away to the landfill as they had been doing.[2]

A congregation in Detroit began offering a free meal on the last five days of the month when the already stretched budget of low-income families refused to stretch any further. When at first only children from the community came, employed members of the congregation began coming so that the parents of the children would hear that they would not be the only adults present. A community of support developed.

Farmers and business persons from a small town in the Midwest joined together when they began receiving word that their homes would be taken away from them because they were unable to pay the rent or the mortgage installments. They learned through legal counsel that they had certain rights of which they had not been aware. Working with creditors they were able to stave off many foreclosures and evictions.

One big difference between the present economic crisis and those of the past (including the depression of the thirties) is that many people today have the conviction things will never be the same again. The need to retrain people whose jobs have been eliminated brings with it the need to encourage them to believe that they can do something different, that life can take on new meaning. Some churches post jobs on a narthex bulletin board as they become known to members. In one congregation all the members who were employers were brought together in order to be appraised of fellow members out of work and to share their expertise in helping the unemployed to find employment. Other churches provide periodic job clinics to enable the unemployed to analyze their own skills, write resumes, and respond to interview situations.

Perhaps the greatest need of people who have become unemployed is the assurance that they are still loved, accepted, and respected. Self-respect and self-worth are severely damaged when someone who has been accustomed to working or who would like to work is unemployed. This was why the parents of hungry children in Detroit at first did not come to the free meals the church offered.

Support groups for the unemployed wherein people meet for Bible study, sermon application, prayer, or conversation with members or persons who are employed can become priorities in congregations moving toward a daily-work-oriented church. Moreover, as society changes in response to the pressures of automation and the world market, the church itself can be a support group for those who work toward the arriving kingdom and who desire equality. The entire membership can become a social-ministry committee, one that can have evangelism by-products. Such church work may be quite different from the traditional "in-house" kind that focuses only on ushering, singing in the choir, and teaching Sunday school. However, it is still church work, a kind that focuses on where most members are during the week.

Two Implications

Traditional ecclesiastical concentration on hierarchical authority is more an example of conforming to managerial practice than an example of being transformed. The first implication is that a truly new church superstructure will emerge only if the managerial tree in the church hierarchy is turned upside down the way it is in those corporations that are in the early hours of Reformation II. Theoretically, one might say that we would simply be substituting one standard of conformity for another, but the differences between the two standards is the difference between God's kingdom priorities announced in Christ and what some call the "Harvard Business School trickle down."

It is probably true, unfortunately, that most of the clergy who are in positions of power in the organizational hierarchy of the church have a left-brain orientation. They have risen to their positions because of the power they project and the authoritarian air that exudes from their personalities. In the interest of moving the church toward democracy and equality, it would be helpful if a right-brain inclination was one of the criteria for determining the qualifications of a theological school graduate who had aspirations for the parish ministry.

It is ironic that right at the time when there is a trend in society toward participation in decision making, some church bodies are seeking to identify their top management position by the title of "bishop." We have alluded to a directive of Jesus that his followers were to serve people rather than lord it over them. In another passage, one that is seldom uttered or quoted, he stipulated that his followers were to use no titles in referring to each other, titles such as rabbi, father, or master. (See Matthew 23:1-12.) Thus, ecclesiastical authorities have a precedent in Scripture that raises some serious questions about such contemporary titles as "pastor," "priest," or "bishop," to say nothing of the title "pope." When clergy persons greet each other, they usually do so on a first name basis. The body of Christ then comes apart when one enters a congregation only to find that titles are in force, along with other marks of distinction and adulation.

Regardless of the official policy, most Protestant churches are really functionally congregational: the local church is the primary unit. What is happening at other levels is out of sight for most lay members of the church.[3] Thus, the "hierarchy" is an elite group of human beings, which relates to a very small segment of the church, even though in many denominations it renders decisions that affect all of the members. It would be an ironic situation if the reformation in the workplace were to have an impact on the congregations but leave the superstructure in the church unreformed.

The second implication, and my conclusion to this theology of work, is that there is only one kingdom and it is the same for everybody. As Jesus said, "You have only one Master and all of you are brothers [and sisters]" (Matthew 23:10).[4] When Jesus spoke of God's kingdom coming and God's will being done on earth *as it is* in heaven, he was saying to us that God's will for life on earth is the same as God's will in eternity. Thus, the church is not a little enclave inside the kingdom that operates on a wavelength that is different from the world around it. Indeed, a realm that is all around us and within us cannot be split into two kingdoms. Such geographical locating might relate to the church building, but it has no relevance for the vast majority of the people who comprise the church, whose weekday life is in the world, not in the church building.

Thus, the laity need not translate grace into justice or commandment keeping, for grace is the heart of justice and is as necessary at work on Monday as in church on Sunday. When it is said that the grace shared in Word and sacrament on Sunday should be thought of on Monday as justice, it loses something in the translation, and so does justice and so does God. The heart of the divine will for all people is left in a church building. Justice can be done without our knowing God, but unmerited grace cannot be shared without knowing God, and there is more to God's kingdom than the equalization of material privileges, as important as this may be for divine credibility. The grace that lies at the heart of justice and equality needs to be shared with others, right along with justice and equality, so that all will know that the kingdom is God's and not a sociological phenomenon, or a classless society that somehow has dawned upon the human scene, or an evolution of history that has occured. God's pressure for justice in the world is really grace at work to make the merit-oriented humble—before God—and the unmerited grateful—to God.

Although at first grace means more to the losers than to the winners in society, in the long run it is the salvation of both, for it results in sharing compassion, recognition of God, and the security that life on this planet needs to survive.

Conversation Starters

The church is a natural place to make connections between grace and weekday work. Do you agree or disagree? Why?

People do not need lengthy input to respond; all they need is the opportunity. Do you agree or disagree? Why?

There is more to grace than a five-minute conclusion to a sermon. Do you agree or disagree? Why?

In a climate of pious platitudes, why does self-honesty convey the grace of God?

In what ways are preparation for and discussion of a sermon a part of the sermon?

"Tools of the trade" have no place on the altar in a church. Do you agree or disagree? Why?

Conversation in the church narthex may have little to do with the sermon, but a lot to do with the grace of God. Do you agree or disagree? Why?

Support groups in the church that focus on daily work concerns have nothing to do with the mission of the church. Do you agree or disagree? Why?

If Reformation II is going to occur in the church, it would be well to make right-brain orientation one of the criterion for pastors. Do you agree or disagree? Why?

Titles for human beings are alien to the mind of Christ and detrimental to the arrival of his kingdom. Do you agree or disagree? Why?

Notes

Preface

[1] Gustaf Wingren, *Creation and Gospel: The New Situation of European Theology* (New York: Edwin Mellen Press, 1979), p. 51.

Chapter 1

[1] Paul's thinking here comes from Romans 7:7-25 and Galations 5.

[2] Roland H. Bainton, *Here I Stand: A Life of Martin Luther* (Nashville: Abingdon Press, 1950), p. 277.

[3] Abraham H. Maslow, "A Theory of Human Motivation," *Psychological Review* (July 1943), pp. 370-396.

[4] In *Luther, an Introduction to His Thought* (London: Collins, 1970), pp. 186-189, Gerhard Ebeling indicates how Luther's kingdom of the left hand encompases secular rule, whereas in the kingdom of the right hand—shared through the church—God dwells, not leaving things up to human intermediaries such as father, mother, emperor, king, or executioner.

[5] In *Principles of Lutheran Theology* (Philadelphia: Fortress Press, 1983), pp. 133-134. Carl Braaten speaks of "modes of divine activity." The "left" means that "God is universally at work in human life through structures and principles commonly operative in political, economic, and cultural institutions that affect the life of all." "Incognito" is our word for what he is saying.

[6] The term "Real Presence" appears frequently in the *Book of Concord* in conjunction with the Lord's Supper. However, in the "Formula of Concord" in that book (Philadelphia: Fortress Press, 1959), p. 587:100, "this presence, as is true of God also, we cannot feel, measure, or comprehend."

[7] William Ophuls, *Ecology and the Politics of Scarcity: Prologue to a Political Theory of the Steady State* (San Francisco: W.H. Freeman Co., Publishers, 1977), p. 237.

133

[8] Benjamin Franklin, "Advice to a Young Tradesman," *Works of Benjamin Franklin*, Vol. II, ed. Jared Sparks (Boston: Whittemore, Niles, and Hall, 1856), p. 88.

[9] Max Weber, *The Protestant Ethic and the Spirit of Capitalism* (New York: Charles Scribner's Sons, 1958), p. 177.

[10] *Ibid.*, p. 197.

[11] *Ibid.*, p. 162.

[12] *Ibid.*, p. 238.

[13] This study was published in 1981 under the title *The Connecticut Mutual Life Report on American Values in the '80s: The Impact of Belief.* Credulity is strained, however, when the Overview notes on page 25 that blue-collar workers, blacks, the least educated, and women are just as enthusiastic about their work as the rest of America.

[14] Adam Smith, author of *The Wealth of Nations*, is regarded by many as the founder of modern economics. He believed that supply and demand results in social harmony, and that this occurs without conscious control or direction "as if by an invisible hand."

[15] *Luther's Works*, vol. 40, *Church and Ministry II* (Philadelphia: Muhlenberg, 1959), pp. 19-20. Luther writes that "it is not enough for anyone who follows Christ to be anointed in order to become a priest. To say that outward ceremonies make a priest . . . is to make no one a priest until he denies that he was a priest before. Thus in the very act of making him a priest they in fact remove him from his priesthood."

[16] Bainton, *Here I Stand*, p. 234.

[17] *Luther's Works*, vol. 45, *The Christian in Society II* (Philadelphia: Muhlenberg, 1962), p. 91. Even though Luther writes that Christians are simultaneously sinners and saints, he still speaks here of the "wicked" outnumbering the "good."

[18] Weber, *The Protestant Ethic*, p. 80.

[19] Frederick Winslow Taylor, *Principles of Scientific Management* (New York: Harper & Row, Publishers, Inc., 1911), pp. 41-47.

[20] John Simmons and William J. Mares, *Working Together* (New York: Alfred A. Knopf, Inc., 1983), p. 16.

[21] Taylor, *Principles*, p. 7.

[22] V.I. Lenin, *Collected Works*, vol. 27, *The Immediate Tasks of the Soviet Government* (Moscow: Progress Publishers, 1965), p. 259. In Russia today the effect of Taylor's "time and motion" is even present on the beaches of resort cities. A large black scoreboard, visible from everywhere on the beach, gives up-to-the-minute information on air and water temperature so bathers know exactly how many minutes of sun, shade, and swimming they can have. Soviet-style hedonism is not an art but a science, according to Donald Kimelman ("A Day at the Beach—Soviet-style," *Philadelphia Inquirer* [August 29, 1983], p. 1).

[23] This comes from the King James Version. Other translations speak of a "large" or "great" crowd who listened eagerly, causing us to assume that among such a throng would be "common" or ordinary people.

Chapter 2

[1] These words appear in all settings for Holy Communion in *The Lutheran Book of Worship* published by various Lutheran Church bodies in America.

[2] This bulletin survey was done in conjunction with the "Affirmations of Faith" study by the Lutheran Church in America in 1973, described in the Preface.

[3] See "Carol Burnett," *Philadelphia Inquirer* (September 2, 1983), p. 8C.

[4] Andrew Hacker, "Creating American Inequality," *New York Review* (March 20, 1980), p. 27.

[5] Joan Beck, "Budget has a little for everyone," *Philadelphia Inquirer* (March 3, 1982).

[6] The questions responded to appeared in the second round of the "Lutheran Listening Post," a study described in more detail in the Preface.

[7] Margaret Kirk, "Can the Main Line Be Saved?" *Today,* the *Philadelphia Inquirer* magazine (April 11, 1982), pp. 10-14, 20, 29.

[8] Beth B. Hess, "New Faces of Poverty," *American Demographics* (May 1983), pp. 26-30. Reprinted with permission. Copyright American Demographics, May 1983.

[9] David Bleakley, *In Place of Work . . . The Sufficient Society* (London: SCM Press, 1981), p. 59.

[10] *Ibid.,* p. 58.

[11] Beverly Norman, "Career Burnout," *Black Enterprise* (July 1981), p. 45.

[12] Elliot Liebow, "Penny Capitalism on an Urban Street Corner," *Anthropology '81/'82* (Guilford Conn.: The Dushkin Publishing Group, 1981), p. 108.

[13] *Ibid.*

Chapter 3

[1] This conference occured in Milwaukee, Wis., in June 1982. The observation appeared in the *Religion and Labor Newsletter* published on that occasion.

[2] William E. Diehl, "A Theology for Supervisors?" *Lutheran Forum* (Pentecost 1980), p. 32.

[3] The article was written by Henry Allen of the *Washington Post* but appeared in the *Philadelphia Inquirer* (October 5, 1981).

[4] Studs Terkel, *Working* (New York: Pantheon Books, 1974), p. 260.

[5] This parable by Clarence Jordan, with the analogy to Uncle Sam, is on a recording labeled "The Great Banquet and Other Parables," recorded in Tiskilwa, Ill., by Koinonia Records.

[6] Shared in an address by William M. Batten at the Wharton School, University of Pennsylvania, 1979. The address was entitled, "Productivity and the Working Environment."

[7] Peter Binzen, "Poll: Bosses fail to back work ethic," *Philadelphia Inquirer* (September 5, 1983), p. 1A.

[8] The words "paid the penalty for" appear nowhere in the New Testament. The idea, however, is implicit in the use of the words "expiation for our sins" in Romans 3:25, Hebrews 2:17, and 1 John 2:2. In Romans Paul declared that God initiated the expiation. It came "from" or "out of" God, which is the meaning of the prefix "ex-." It was not paid to God; it was not propitiation or appeasement.

[9] In Galations 3:13 Paul wrote that Christ became a curse for us, and in 2 Corinthians 5:18 Paul wrote, "All this is from God, who through Christ reconciled us to himself."

Chapter 4

[1] Lance Morrow, "What Is the Point of Working?" *Time* (May 11, 1981), p. 93.

[2] David Bleakley, *In Place of Work . . . The Sufficient Society* (London: SCM Press, 1981), p. 95.

[3] Ronald Fraser, ed., *Work: Twenty Personal Accounts* (New York: Penguin Books, 1968), pp. 99, 103.

[4] *Ibid.,* p. 12.

[5] Margaret Kane, *Gospel in Industrial Society* (London: SCM Press, 1980), pp. 44-45.

[6] Bleakley, *In Place of Work,* p. 94.

[7] Morrow, *Time*, p. 93.
[8] William H. Willimon, "A Labor Day Reflection on the Work Ethic," *The Christian Century* (August 31–September 7, 1983), p. 778.
[9] John Oliver Nelson, ed., *Work and Vocation: A Christian Discussion* (New York: Harper & Row, Publishers, Inc., 1954), pp. 156-157.
[10] Dietrich Bonhoeffer, *Life Together* (New York: Harper & Row, Publishers, Inc., 1954), p. 27.
[11] *Ibid.*, pp. 27, 31.

Chapter 5

[1] Stuart Chase, *Men at Work* (New York: Harcourt Brace Jovanovich, Inc., 1944), p. 37.
[2] From a filmstrip, "Let's Face It!" prepared by the Division of Christian Education of the American Baptist Convention and based on research by Richard Myers.
[3] John Simmons and William J. Mares, *Working Together* (New York: Alfred A. Knopf, Inc., 1983), p. 43.
[4] *Ibid.*, p. 99.
[5] Milton Derber, *The American Idea of Industrial Democracy* (Urbana: University of Illinois Press, 1970), pp. 469-470.
[6] Douglas McGregor, *The Human Side of Enterprise* (New York: McGraw-Hill, Inc., 1960), p. 113.
[7] *Ibid.*, pp. 33-34, 47-48.
[8] James O'Toole, ed., *Work and the Quality of Life: Resource Papers for Work in America* (Cambridge, Mass.: MIT Press, 1974), p. 13. This consists of sixteen papers prepared for a study published in 1973 under the title *Work in America*.
[9] Emma Rothschild, *Paradise Lost—The Decline of the Auto-Industrial Age* (New York: Random House, Inc., Vintage Books, 1974), p. 119.
[10] Simmons and Mares, *Working Together*, p. 160.
[11] *Ibid.*, p. 212.
[12] Tom Richman, "Mister Megatrend," *Inc.* (January 1983), p. 00.
[13] Quoted in Simmons and Mares, *Working Together*, p. 102.
[14] *Ibid.*, p. 110.
[15] Jim Fuller, "Workers Gaining Voice in Job Policy," Minneapolis *Tribune* (July 8, 1979), p. 1D. Cited in Simmons and Mares, *Working Together*, p. 16.
[16] Simmons and Mares, *Working Together*, p. 160.
[17] Derber, *The American Idea*, p. 470.
[18] Ronald Reagan, on the radio program "Viewpoint," February 1975. Cited in Simmons and Mares, *Working Together*, pp. 127-128.
[19] Simmons and Mares, *Working Together*, p. 101.
[20] Milton Fisk, "Economic Justice," quoted in Tom L. Beauchamp and Norman E. Bowie, *Ethical Theory and Business* (Englewood Cliffs, N.J.: Prentice-Hall, Inc.), pp. 631-632.
[21] Simmons and Mares, *Working Together*, p. 215.
[22] David K. Easlick, "To See Ourselves as Others See Us," *Bell Telephone Magazine*, no. 4, 1980, pp. 20-21.
[23] Simmons and Mares, *Working Together*, p. 204.
[24] Pehr Gyllenhammar, *People at Work* (Reading, Mass.: Addison-Wesley Publishing Co., Inc., 1977), p. 162.
[25] Simmons and Mares, *Working Together*, pp. 204-205.
[26] *Ibid.*, p. 215.
[27] Daniel Zwerdling, *Workplace Democracy* (New York: Harper & Row, Publishers, Inc., 1979), p. 27.

[28] *Ibid.*

[29] Simmons and Mares, *Working Together*, p. 283.

[30] Michael Maccoby, *The Leader: A New Face for American Management* (New York: Simon & Schuster, Inc., 1981), p. 234.

[31] *Ibid.*, p. 223.

[32] James F. Lincoln, *A New Approach to Industrial Economics* (New York: Devin-Adair, Co., Inc., 1961), p. 22.

Chapter 6

[1] George Katona, *Psychological Economics* (New York: American Elsevier Publishers, Inc., 1975), pp. 140, 189-191.

[2] Jeremiah used this phrase in Lamentations 3:23. Also, in 2 Corinthians 4:16 Paul wrote that while our outer, physical nature is wasting away, our inner nature is being renewed every day.

[3] C. G. Montefiore and H. Loewe, ed., *A Rabbinic Anthology* (New York: Schocken Books, Inc., 1978), pp. 223-224. Reprinted by permission of Schocken Books, Inc., from *A Rabbinic Anthology*, C. G. Montefiore and H. Loewe, editors. First Schocken edition 1974.

[4] For an extended treatment of this parable along the line indicated here, see James Breech, *The Silence of Jesus: The Authentic Voice of the Historical Man* (Philadelphia: Fortress Press, 1983), pp. 150-155.

[5] Mary Walton, "Making America Work Again," *Philadelphia Inquirer* (March 11, 1984), pp. 20-27.

[6] John Simmons and William J. Mares, *Working Together* (New York: Alfred A. Knopf, Inc., 1983), p. 214.

[7] "Steel Jacks Up Its Productivity," *Business Week* (October 12, 1981), p. 86.

[8] Walton, "Making America Work Again" p. 25.

[9] Jim Fuller, "Workers Gaining Voice in Job Policy," Minneapolis *Tribune* (July 8, 1979), p. 1D. Cited in Simmons and Mares, *Working Together*, p. 161.

[10] In the "Smalcald Articles" (*Book of Concord*, p. 310) this appears alongside "preaching" and the "sacraments," but not separate from "absolution." Although "mutual conversation" is the way "consolation" would be conveyed, in *The Theology of Martin Luther* (Philadelphia, Fortress Press, 1966, p. 318) Paul Althaus observes how "mutual conversation" widens the scope to such a degree that the total association of the Christian with his brothers and sisters is involved when the need is for comfort or advice. This is hardly confined to the narthex of a church building on Sunday morning or to activities in that building during the week.

[11] David Hoekema, "The State of Nature: Reagan and Hobbes," *The Christian Century* (May 6, 1981), p. 501.

[12] Simmons and Mares, *Working Together*, pp. 209-210.

[13] Joseph Spieler, "After the Recession," *Quest* (September 1980), p. 28.

[14] Bruce Nussbaum, "Reskilling Workers," *New York Times* (June 12, 1983), 19E.

[15] From abstract of Barry O. Jones, *Sleepers, Wake! Technology and the Future of Work* (Melbourne and New York: Oxford University Press, 1983), in *Future Survey* (July 1983), p. 5.

[16] David Bleakley, *In Place of Work . . . The Sufficient Society* (London: SCM Press, 1981), p. 82.

[17] Dietrich Bonhoeffer, *Ethics* (New York: Macmillan, Inc., 1965), p. 64.

[18] Dietrich Bonhoeffer, *Letters and Papers from Prison* (London: SCM Press, 1953), p. 104.

[19] H. Richard Niebuhr, *The Meaning of Revelation* (New York: Macmillan, Inc., 1941), p. 126.

20 Austin Farrer, *The Glass of Vision* (London: Dacre Press, 1948), p. 31.

Chapter 7

1 Edouard Beauduin, "Faith, The Principal Requirement of Christian Unity," *Lumen Vitae*, no. 23 (1968), p. 25.

2 Robert Benne, *The Ethic of Democratic Capitalism: A Moral Reassessment* (Philadelphia: Fortress Press, 1981), p. 150.

3 Dennis Little, "Post-Industrial Society and What It May Mean," *The Futurist* (December 1973), p. 261.

4 "How Consumers Spend," *American Demographics* (October 1983), p. 17.

5 In Galatians 5:19-21 these sins are listed along with others, though the reference to their being deadly did not surface until centuries later.

6 In his chapter analyzing the Lutheran data in *Ministry in Amercia* (San Francisco: Harper & Row, Publishers, Inc., 1980), p. 439, George Lindback further writes, on page 438, "A normative rhetoric prescribes the character and possibilities of reform. It provides the standards and directives within which renewal takes place when and if consciences are awakened and circumstances are favorable."

7 Tom Richman, "Mister Megatrend," *Inc.* (January 1983), p. 3.

8 Michael D. Wuchter, "Disarmament in a Nuclear Age," Aim Series, produced by the Division for Parish Services of the Lutheran Church in America in Philadelphia.

9 Paul speaks of this in 1 Corinthians 3:11.

10 Robert Lekachman, "Supply Side Economics: Is It Fair? Can It Succeed?" Contemporary Social Issue publication, Spring 1982, Lutheran Church in America's Division for Mission to North America.

Chapter 8

1 Weston H. Agor, "Tomorrow's Intuitive Leaders," *The Futurist* (August 1983), pp. 49-51.

2 "Urban Newsletter," vol. 14, no. 3 (September 1983), a publication of the Lutheran Church in America's Division for Parish Services.

3 "Alban Institute Action Information" (May-June 1983), p. 4.

4 Matthew 23:10. Even if a verse such as this were a product of the early church, it does not exactly run counter to the mind of Christ or to exalting Jesus as the head of the church, as is done in other places in the New Testament.

Index

126, 130
Communication, 62, 77, 99
Communism, 25, 78, 109-111, 113
Competition, 12, 41, 48, 50, 64, 70, 72, 122
Computer, 95-98, 108
Conflict, 26, 62
Cooperation, 70-73
Creation, 31, 50, 55, 58, 103, 106, 115
Creator, 31-33, 35, 37, 40, 57-58, 64-65, 103, 105-106, 111, 114-115
Crime, 108
Cross, 51-53, 114

Dana Corporation, 75, 77, 91-92
Dangerfield, Rodney, 75
Davis, Harvey, 76-77
Declaration of Independence, 32, 40
Deming, W. Edwards, 72, 90-92
Democracy, 48, 77, 79-80, 82, 129
Denka, 77
Discussion, 61, 70, 119-120, 123
Duty, 24-25

Easlick, David (Michigan Bell Telephone), 79
Education, 10, 26, 32, 34, 70, 74, 77, 93, 97, 108, 120
Edwards, Jonathan, 20
Efficiency, 42-43, 46-47, 80, 83
Employees, 39, 48, 72, 75-78, 84, 95, 127
Employers, 24, 39, 52, 95, 128
Environment, 32
Equality, 32-33, 65, 83, 88, 94, 105-109; and Jesus, 114-115; church and, 129; belief in, 104, 111; economic, 105; God and, 114; grace and, 131; of opportunity, 102-103; Paul and, 116; sharing, 131.
Erving, Julius, 63
Eucharist, 124
Experience: as participants, 11,

104; as preacher, 9; daily, 41, 49, 55; democratic, 80-81; disillusioning and humbling, 37-38; in church and work, 11, 19; of Jesus, as a carpenter, 26, 124; of Christian fellowship, 66; of Paul, 89, 93, 122; the gospel, 64

Factory, 12, 15-16, 34, 56, 58-59, 73, 96-98
Faith, 11, 29-30, 37, 53, 59, 61, 63, 66, 93, 110, 115-116; and economic benefits, 109; and physical needs, 18; and reality, 27; awareness, 51; Christian, 11, 19, 109; effect of work ethic on, 30; fear in place of, 93; in technology, 25; Jesus and, 26, 114-115; meaning of, 10; of "founding fathers," 32; principle of, 49; relevance of, 12; talking about, 119
Fall, The, 55-58
Farmers, 17, 46-47, 90, 128
Favoritism, 21, 33
Fear, 17, 39, 50, 79, 91-92, 107
Ferraro, Geraldine, 33
Forgiveness, 17, 40, 52, 61, 92
Ford Motor Company, 10, 46, 71, 77
Fortune magazine, 48
Franklin, Ben, 20
Free enterprise, 40, 94

Gallup, George, 37
Gandhi, 63
General Foods, 74-75, 81-82
General Motors, 71, 75, 98
Genetics, 31-32, 102-103, 106, 108
God, 11, 15, 19-24, 26-27, 34-38, 40-41, 45, 49-53, 55-56, 60, 62-63, 65-67, 85-89, 92, 98-100, 101-104, 109-111, 113-115, 119-122, 126, 132; the Creator, 31-33, 57-58, 63-65, 103, 105-106; generosity of, 44, 89; left

143